Ann Crozier's
PASSION FOR PERSIMMONS

A Collection of 87 Persimmon Recipes
with Commentary by the Author

Copyright © 2009 Ojai Valley Library Friends & Foundation
ISBN 978-1-4507-0388-8

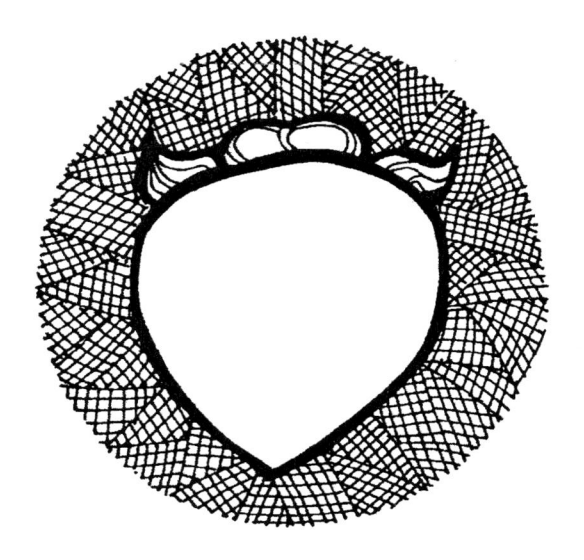

Each orb some light left from summer
Glowing on brown fall ground
The persimmons are flowing
                    Gary Snyder

TABLE OF CONTENTS

INTRODUCTION AND PROCESSING NOTES   7

APPETIZERS   13

BREADS   21

SOUPS   31

SALADS AND SALAD DRESSINGS   41

SAUCES, SALSAS, CHUTNEYS AND JAMS   57

DESSERTS   63

AND NOW, THE COOKIES!   79

ACKNOWLEDGMENTS   87

ABOUT THE AUTHOR   89

ABOUT THE AUTHOR ~ BY THE AUTHOR   91

ABOUT THE ILLUSTRATOR   93

RECIPE INDEX   95

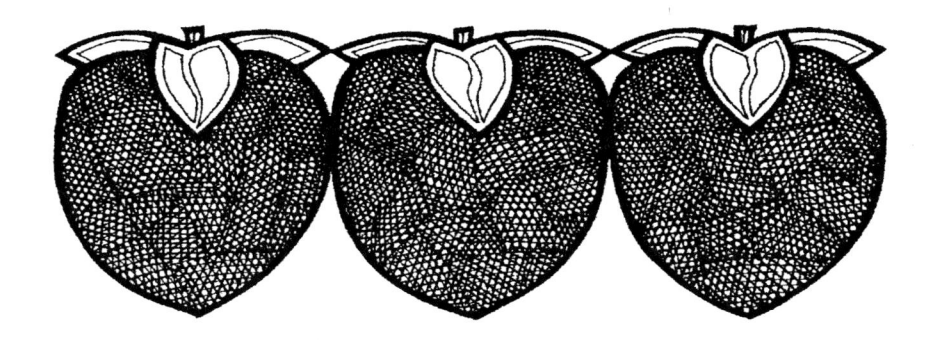

INTRODUCTION AND PROCESSING NOTES

In the beginning there were the persimmon trees. Two of them, big shady trees with heart-shaped leaves that turned beautifully red and gold in the fall and produced bountiful copious crops of bright orange fruit – hundreds and hundreds every November. The trees were probably planted in the 1950s when my house in Ojai, California, was built. They are tall for fruit trees, about 25 feet, and eventually I learned that one is called a *Hachiya* and the other a *Fuyu*.

The *Hachiya* persimmon must be very ripe before it's ready to eat – the consistency of soft mushy jam. It's the persimmon with the pointed end. The *Fuyu* can be eaten when still hard and crisp. These are the two main varieties of *Diospyros kaki* grown both commercially and in home orchards in the U.S. There are hundreds of other varieties available in the Orient where persimmons are much revered.

That reverence is not shared here in Ojai, where persimmons get little respect or attention. And it's easy to understand why. The *Hachiya* is the most commonly available and its fruit is astringent unless eaten dead ripe, ripe almost to the point of looking rotten. And even if you get past this, the flavor is, well, not much. It's sweet but insipidly so. (Yes, you just read this in a persimmon cookbook!)

Still, I found the trees beautiful. They are disease resistant and drought tolerant and they attract many birds, which stand out against the bare branches in the winter and thus are easy to watch and identify. For years I just watched the birds enjoy the fruit. I was busy with other things, although I did do a bit of baking. My friend Dorothy Rail shared her recipe for persimmon cookies. They were delicious, but the recipe used only one persimmon. I had (some years at least) what seemed like thousands.

The neighborhood boasted other persimmon trees, each laden with hundreds of fruit ripening on the tree in the fall. They were still there sometimes until January or even February – big, luscious crops one cannot give away at any time of the year.

Persimmons are the zucchini of the backyard fruit orchard. They needed a cookbook! Dorothy's cookies were good, but surely there were other recipes one could try. I began to experiment and learned that the essential flavor of the persimmon is sweet but ineffably shy, and it will lend itself to endless variations. This bland quality becomes a virtue the cook can play with.

I also learned that persimmons are very nutritious, full of vitamin A as well as C. They also are good sources of beta-carotene and potassium and are relatively low in calories – 70 per serving, about two-thirds of a persimmon. They are NOT, as my friend Karen McAuley told me, "just sugar."

Most recipes for persimmons in other cookbooks are for desserts. I tried many desserts but also salad dressings, sauces, soups and breads, especially yeast breads. I found that persimmons also can be dried, and then I discovered that *Fuyu* persimmons can be roasted. In each case, the flavor changes. One important point: be careful when cooking with the *Hachiya*. When heated, the fruit may revert to the astringency it loses as it ripens. This is why one cannot make *Hachiya* persimmon chutney or jam that is cooked for a long period of time. On the other hand, persimmon pulp works fine in soups. Go figure.

I have had a lot of fun experimenting and I urge you to experiment yourself. I have used recipes featuring a large variety of fruits and vegetables for inspiration. These include pumpkin, parsnips, sweet potatoes, carrots, apricots, apples, papayas, pears, figs, dates and mangoes. How many other fruits could make this claim?

Though shy, persimmons are wonderfully adaptive and versatile. I began to eye the huge crop of ripening fruit with anticipation and, yes, even joy and, it's true, with passion! I hope I can share some of that feeling with you.

INGREDIENTS

I've been interested in oriental cooking for a number of years, and many of my recipes reflect that. Sweet-sour flavors are ubiquitous in this cuisine. The naturally sweet persimmon is mixed with tart lime or lemon or combined with fish sauce or tamarind. This is not too traditional, but it works!

Chinese chili paste often appears in my recipes as well. Recently, I've been experimenting with the wonderful deep flavors of Japanese miso paste. It gives a subtle tang to soups and salad dressings. All these ingredients are available at oriental markets – and often you can find them at large supermarkets. I've found both chili paste and fish sauce addictive, and you may also find their funky flavors appealing. I hope so. I am also especially taken with ginger – as you will see when you read the recipes. Some call for fresh ginger, but much of my baking features preserved crystallized ginger. This you can find at *Trader Joe's* as well as at larger markets.

PROCESSING

Most of my recipes call for different amounts of strained fruit. My persimmons are usually fairly large, but persimmons vary in size, so many of the recipes require explicit amounts of strained pulp, rather than one or two or three persimmons. As a general rule, one persimmon equals ¼ cup of strained fruit. The pulp freezes beautifully. I save small plastic containers and freeze the pulp in them. It will keep for up to a year – until the new crop is ripe. You also can freeze persimmon pulp in ice cube trays, measuring 1or 2 tablespoons of fruit into each compartment, freezing the pulp, storing the frozen cubes in plastic bags and then using the pre-measured fruit in recipes that call for small amounts.

To process, strain the fruit through a colander or mesh strainer. For me the colander works best. I position it over a large bowl and push the whole persimmons through and discard the skins and seeds left in the colander. The experience has the same squishy feel as messing with kindergarten finger paint. Be sure your persimmons are dead ripe – very soft and of jelly consistency. To ripen fast, place them overnight in your freezer or in a plastic bag with an apple.

My recipes for yeast breads and some cakes simply call for persimmon pulp – persimmons processed in a food processor without this process of straining the fruit. This is easier, but watch out for stray seeds that may turn up in the batter as you proceed with the recipe.

DRYING PERSIMMONS

I was thrilled when I discovered dried persimmons. I learned recently that the word persimmon is a variation of a Native American word meaning dried fruit – thus demonstrating the Native American wisdom that once dried, the persimmon comes into its own. (Its botanical name, *Diospyros kaki*, means fruit of the gods. I'm not the only one passionate about persimmons!) There are several ways to dry them and each produces fruit with different texture and taste. I like them all, but I prefer what I call the string method. This method is used in Japan where whole dried persimmons are called *Hoshigaki*. String drying is labor intensive at first, but you can keep the strings from one year to the next and the work involved quickly becomes something you can do while watching the evening news or listening to NPR. The dried fruit has a luscious date-like flavor and chewy consistency that is outstanding. Once you try *Hoshigaki*, you'll understand why the Japanese (and everyone else) love them, and believe me, you'll look at your persimmon tree with more respect.

You must harvest the fruit in a particular way that may sound complicated but isn't. So, here goes:

Arm yourself with a pair of garden hand pruners and find a persimmon tree. The fruit should be bright orange but hard – not at the dead ripe soft jelly consistency of a ripe *Hachiya* persimmon. Clip the fruit from the tree so that a small (one inch or so) amount of stem remains on either side of the fruit and forms a "T." You will use this stem to hang the fruit to dry. Looking at the persimmons on the tree will make these directions clear.

Once you've harvested the fruit (each with their hanging "T"), tie strings to hang each. Either use a long piece of string to tie several fruit together a few inches apart – each secured by their T shaped stem – or tie a loop at each end of a 2-foot piece of string and drape it over a suspended rod or pole. Using a vegetable peeler, peel the fruit, then hang your persimmons under the eaves of your house or garage – or in a shed that is open on all sides. You need good air circulation to minimize the risk of rot. And don't worry about insects bothering the fruit. I've been at it a long time and have never had a problem with this. Give the persimmons 4 to 6 weeks to dry. It takes a while, but the results are worth it.

When they are ready, try not to eat them all at once. The persimmons will keep best if you freeze them once they are dried. You can store them at room temperature, but they will form sugar crystals on the outside. This is harmless but looks a bit like mold. Their appearance is better if frozen. Just put them in plastic bags and store in the freezer. They'll keep beautifully for up to a year.

String-dried persimmons are wonderful eaten out of hand, but they can be used in almost any recipe calling for dates or dried figs. Since they are not quite as sweet, add a little sugar as well. Unless otherwise specified, all of the recipes in this book that call for dry persimmons are written with string-dried fruit in mind.

Persimmons also can be dried using a food dehydrator. The fruit will retain its bright orange color, and the flavor will be much closer to that of the original persimmon. I find that it's best to peel the fruit again, but you don't have to. You do have to slice it about ¼ inch thick. You can start harvesting your fruit for hydrator drying in October, when the fruit is still crisp and easier to slice, and continue to process it through the season. The beautiful persimmon star pattern emerges when you follow this method. After cutting up your fruit, follow the directions for use of your dehydrator. Experiment for the texture you like. I dry mine for about 10 hours.

ROASTING PERSIMMONS

Late in my persimmon adventures, I discovered roasting. The fruit must be the *Fuyu* variety, the bigger the better. Whoever planted my trees selected the Giant *Fuyu* cultivar. Giants are available at farmer's markets. Ask for them. All varieties of *Fuyu* persimmons can be roasted, but you'll get more for your effort with the larger Giants. Roasting really enhances the fruit's flavor. It also makes the fruit keep better, so your dish will make for better leftovers.

For roasting, I recommend peeling the persimmons first, removing the core and seeds, and then slicing them about a ½ inch thick. Now line a baking sheet with aluminum foil, spray the foil with a little canola cooking spray and arrange the slices back to back on the sheets. Spray the fruit with the cooking spray and roast them at 400° for about an hour. Use a spatula to flip the fruit midway in the process. *Fuyus* also can be cut in half, roasted for 30 minutes, then stuffed with some sort of delicious concoction and the roasting process continued for another half an hour or so.

I have found many uses for roasted persimmons and have discovered that if processed this way the fruit freezes beautifully. Just put about 1 cup into individual plastic bags, seal and store together in the freezer. Your fruit can then be used later in the year (if the cook can resist them that long). You will find most of my roasted persimmon recipes in the soup and salad sections of this book, but I continue to find other uses as well.

Ann Crozier
Ojai, California
2008

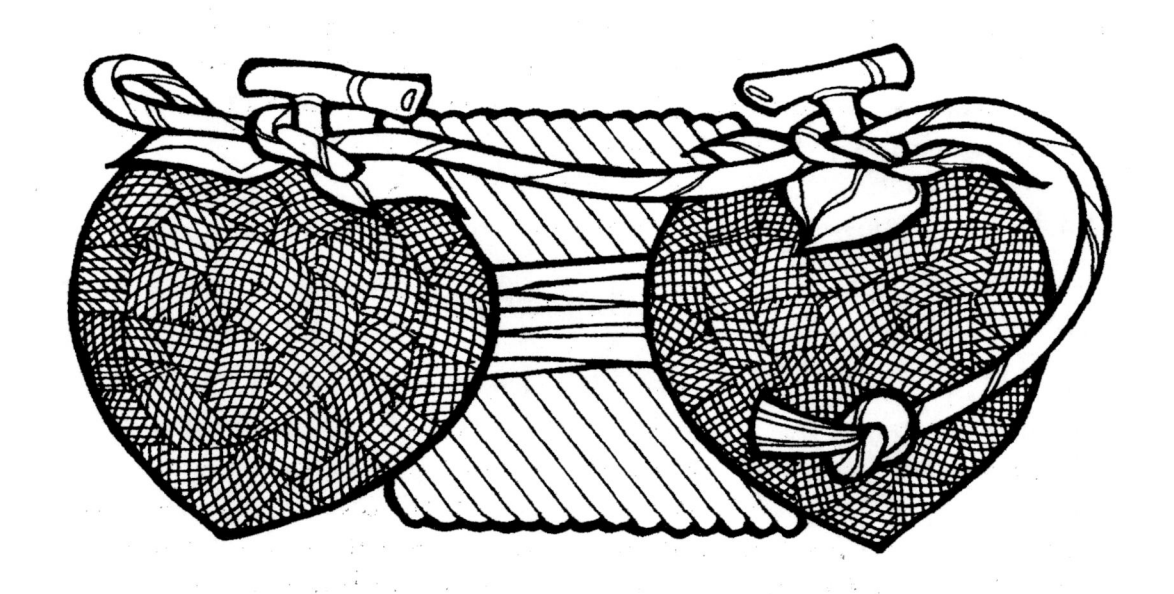

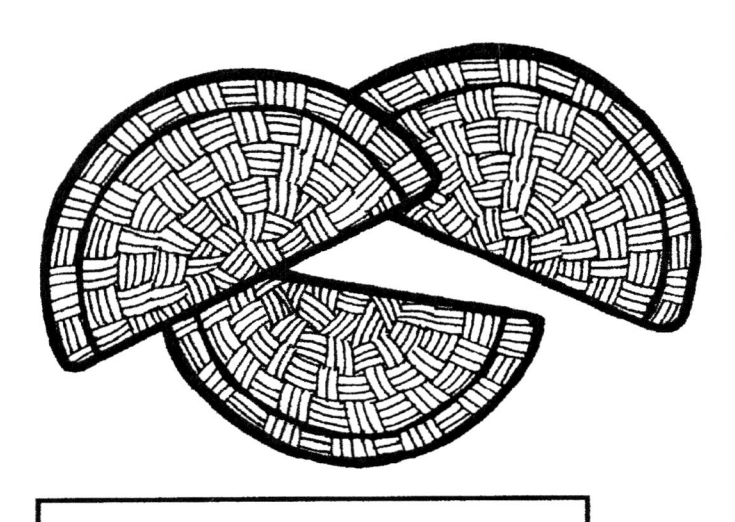

APPETIZERS

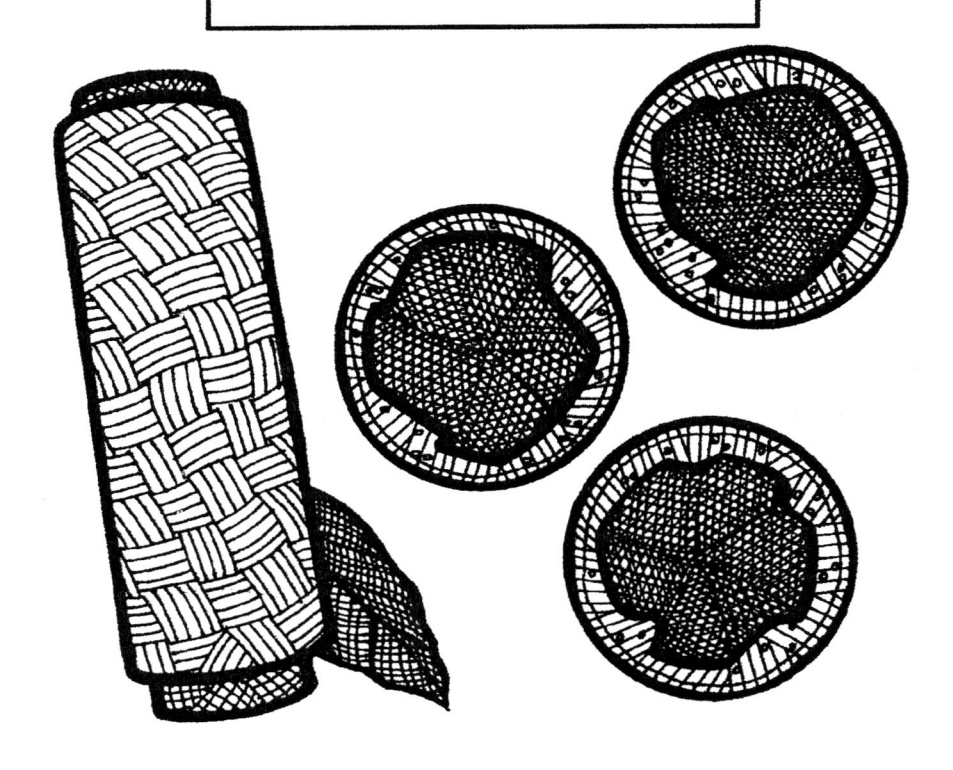

APPETIZERS

I'm a cook (and an eater) who has never seen much need for appetizers. My own appetite never needs enhancement. Never. Well, hardly ever. And therefore I haven't worked too hard at finding appetizer recipes. But sometimes the cook wants to keep her guests happy while she fusses a bit longer in the kitchen. So if you feel the need, here are a few such recipes. This section also features dishes you could serve for lunch.

FRESH *FUYU* PERSIMMONS WITH LIME

This recipe was suggested to me by my good friend Ojai librarian Kit Willis.

2 *Fuyu* persimmons   1 lime

Core the persimmons and remove seeds. Cut them into slices. Squeeze the lime juice over and serve. Simple and elegant!

DRIED PERSIMMONS WITH GOAT CHEESE

These are a little more complicated than the preceding, but not much. This is one of my favorites of the recipes I've collected over the years. You can serve these before a meal or even afterwards on a tray of assorted cookies and other treats. I once visited a small restaurant in Paris where the meal began with what the host called an amuse bouche. Your mouth will truly be amused with these.

6 dried persimmons (string dried)   Chopped pistachios or pecans
Small amount of goat cheese, say   (Pistachios are better)
¼ cup

Cut the persimmons in two and cut out the small core leaving a small cavity. Stuff this with a little wedge of goat cheese and top the cheese with a sprinkling of the chopped nuts. Arrange on a small tray and prepare to amuse some *bouches*.

PERSIMMON HUMMUS

Surprise your guests with this variation on the standard tahini and garbanzo spread. This is easy to make and it also freezes well.

¼ c tahini
1 can of garbanzo beans, drained
1 T plus 1 t minced fresh ginger
1 t salt

¼ c fresh orange juice
¼ c persimmon puree
1 T lime juice

Whirl all ingredients in a blender. Add more salt or fresh ginger to taste. Serve with crackers or veggies as a spread or dip, or use as a sandwich enhancer. Makes about 1½ cups.

PERSIMMON PICKLES

I remember when I visited Japan seeing a food emporium where what seemed like hundreds of different kinds of pickles were sold. I decided to try pickling persimmons. By gum, it worked. These are fun to serve on an appetizer tray alone or with other assorted chopped vegetables. Your guests will be intrigued. The pickles, however, are not for the faint of palate.

5-6 *Fuyu* persimmons, slightly green
1 c cider vinegar
¾ c rice vinegar

⅔ c sugar
1 T finely chopped fresh ginger
½ t dried red chili flakes
1 T kosher salt

Peel persimmons, core and slice them into thin wedges, about ⅓ of an inch wide. Pack in four eight-ounce canning jars. Mix the rest of the ingredients in a medium sauce pan and bring to a simmer. Stir to dissolve sugar and salt. Remove from heat and carefully pour over the fruit. Seal and process in a hot water bath for 10 minutes. Makes 4 small jars of unique pickles.

PERSIMMON PÂTÉ

I based this dish on a fig pâté from Jeremy Jackson's Good Food for a Picnic.

¼ c slivered almonds
1¼ c dried persimmons (string-dried)
1 t anise seed

1 T brandy
1½ t balsamic vinegar
⅛ t freshly ground black pepper

Grind the anise seed in a spice grinder or clean coffee grinder. Cut the persimmons in half and check for any hidden seeds. Place the almonds, dried persimmons, brandy, vinegar and 1½ teaspoons of water in the bowl of a food processor. Process until the mixture is a paste. Add the ground anise and the pepper. Place the persimmon paste on a sheet of aluminum foil and shape it into a rough 6 inch log, then wrap it tightly in the foil, rolling to shape it into a cylinder. Unwrap the foil and place the log – still on the foil – onto a baking sheet. Bake at 200° until the surface of the log dries and hardens a bit, 20 to 25 minutes. Let it cool. Wrap the log in foil and keep in a plastic bag in the refrigerator for up to 2 months. Serve on crackers.

ROASTED PERSIMMON TURNOVERS
WITH ALLSPICE AND ORANGE

These are an interesting labor-intensive dish, time-consuming to make but fun to offer guests. The turnovers can be served as a side dish with a luncheon soup or salad. They are a lot of work but all the prep can be done ahead and the turnovers frozen. I am so taken with roasting Fuyu persimmons that I will roast some for a soup or salad and then save some to freeze for a special dish like this. And you could just make the filling, wrap a tortilla around a bit of it and call it lunch. An excellent lunch at that. I've included an alternate filling as well. Yield as directed is about 20.

TURNOVER DOUGH

2 c all-purpose flour
1 t salt
2/3 c chilled butter cut into 10 pieces

1 large egg, lightly beaten
5 to 6 T cold water

PERSIMMON FILLING

½ c roasted *Fuyu* persimmon, chopped
1 onion, chopped
1 T butter
Half of a sweet red pepper, chopped
½ c slivered almonds
¼ c raisins

1 t salt or to taste
Juice and zest of 1 orange (more zest to taste)
¼ t allspice
½ c mozzarella or jack cheese, grated

EGG WASH

1 egg, lightly beaten   1 T water   ¼ t salt

First, make the dough. Combine the flour and salt in a food processor and pulse to blend. Add the butter and pulse, until the mixture resembles cornmeal. Combine the egg and 5 tablespoons of water. With the machine running, slowly add the egg mixture and process just until roughly combined. If the mixture seems dry, add up to 1 tablespoon more water. Turn out onto a lightly floured board and knead into a rough dough. Wrap in plastic wrap and refrigerate for 30 minutes.

Heat a skillet and add the butter. When it foams, add the onion and sauté until golden – about 5 minutes. Add the pepper and sauté for about a minute. Add the rest of the ingredients, except cheese, and let simmer for a few minutes. Then stir in cheese. Set aside to cool a bit. (For instructions on roasting persimmons, see beginning section of this book. Defrosted roasted persimmons work well here.)

On a lightly floured surface, roll out the dough to a circle that is approximately 1/6-inch thick. Using a 3-inch round cutter, cut out circles from the dough. Place a tablespoon of the persimmon mixture in the center of each dough circle. Lightly moisten the edges with water and fold over to form a half circle, enclosing the filling. Press to seal. Place on a baking sheet. Repeat with remaining dough and filling. Combine the egg wash ingredients and blend well. Brush the tops of the turnovers with the egg wash. Bake in a preheated 400° oven for 20 minutes, or until golden brown. Cool slightly before serving. You will probably have some leftover filling. Roll it up in a tortilla, and call it lunch.

The unbaked turnovers will keep for several months in the freezer. To bake, arrange unthawed on a baking sheet, brush with wash and bake as directed.

ALTERNATE TURNOVER FILLING FEATURING FENNEL AND ANISE

1 t anise seed
½ c fresh orange juice
1 T canola oil
¼ c roasted *Fuyu* persimmon, chopped

1 fennel bulb chopped
1 onion chopped
1 T canola oil
¼ c slivered almonds
½ c shredded mozzarella cheese

In a small saucepan, bring orange juice and anise seed to a slow boil and reduce to ¼ cup. It will take just a minute so watch the pot. Set aside. Heat oil in a medium frying pan and sauté onion and fennel until soft, about 5 minutes. Now add fruit, almonds and juice mixture. Simmer for a minute or two. Remove from heat. Cool and then add cheese. Salt to taste. Use as turnover filling or for a great burrito.

OPEN-FACED CHEESE, ONION AND ROASTED PERSIMMON SANDWICHES

A version of the recipe was one of the Los Angeles Times' Best of the Year candidates a few years ago. I have substituted roasted persimmons for the figs it called for and also tweaked it a couple of other ways. Roasted persimmons and caramelized onions are a dynamite combo. This is a recipe where I assume you have a stash of frozen roasted persimmons. If you don't, see the beginning section of the cookbook and roast some Fuyus.

¼ c sweet wine, such as Muscat
½ c roasted persimmon slices
2 T olive oil
6 c sliced onions
1 t sugar

1 t fresh thyme leaves
1 t salt
4 slices whole grained bread
3 ounces thinly-sliced mozzarella cheese

In a large skillet over medium heat, heat 2 tablespoons of olive oil. Add onions, stir in sugar, thyme and salt. Reduce heat to low, cover and cook until onions are golden brown, about 35 minutes. Uncover and add wine, turn up heat to medium and cook until wine is reduced to syrup – about 5 minutes. Now toast the bread, top each slice with a serving of the onions, some of the roasted persimmon and a little cheese. Heat under a broiler until the cheese has melted and serve immediately. Makes 4 sandwiches.

PERSIMMON SPRING ROLLS WITH PEANUT SAUCE

My sister Susan and I are fond of the spring rolls we discovered at a Ventura Thai restaurant. These are not deep fried, but served with the rice paper dough uncooked and also feature lots of fresh basil. I discovered a similar recipe featuring fresh papaya on the Epicurious web site. I like these with roasted persimmon better. You could try them with fresh Fuyu as well. Fairly easily made and fun to eat . . . these are another appetizer dish that could serve as lunch.

½ c peanut butter
½ c warm water
2 T rice vinegar
2 T fish sauce
1 t chili paste
12 rice paper spring roll squares

36 large fresh basil leaves
1 c roasted persimmon slices, each cut in half
1½ c finely sliced napa cabbage
Cilantro sprigs

For instructions on roasting persimmons, see beginning section of this cookbook.

Whirl peanut sauce ingredients in a food processor and set aside. To assemble spring rolls, place 1 large basil leaf on a spring roll square, top with a small amount of chopped cabbage, top this with some slices of persimmon, a couple of cilantro sprigs and another basil leaf. Fold one end of each square over filling. Fold in ends. Roll up and place on your serving tray. Repeat. Cover with a paper towel, place in plastic bag and refrigerate until serving. Bring peanut sauce to room temperature before serving. Make sure your guests have a napkin.

BREADS

BREADS

I've had a lot of fun experimenting with persimmon breads, especially yeast breads. Persimmon pulp (persimmons that have been put in a food processor and pureed) adds a chewy texture and wonderful color to many yeast breads. Surprisingly, the sweetness is very subtle, the persimmon flavor recedes, and the breads can be flavored in a variety of unorthodox ways. Feel confident with substituting persimmon puree for any baking recipe that calls for pumpkin, but try other things as well.

The best thing about these breads, other than their wonderful flavor and unusual texture, is that they use a lot of persimmons (a goal for any persimmon tree owner.) And with most of the yeast breads, you don't have to strain the fruit, just puree it in a food processor and measure out two cups – about four persimmons. But watch out for any stray seeds. They'll turn up when you knead the bread.

But please note: None of these recipes are configured for a bread machine. I love to knead bread, so I persist with antiquated methods. Slow down, spend the day at home and savor the process. It takes a while, but you are not tied to the kitchen, just check in occasionally. The results are worth it.

All of these breads freeze beautifully. They'll keep up to six months in the freezer. And you'll have lots to share with your pals or for unusual gifts.

PERSIMMON ANISE BREAD

2 c water
2 c persimmon pulp, unstrained
(about 4 persimmons, skin & all)
1 T anise seed
1½ T dry yeast

1 T sugar
1 T salt
3½ c whole wheat flour
3–4 c bread or unbleached all purpose flour
1 c raisins (optional)

Bring 1 cup of water to a boil. Add the 1 tablespoon of anise seed and remove pan from heat. Let this mixture cool to lukewarm. Meanwhile, in a large mixing bowl proof the yeast in the other cup of warm water. Add sugar and yeast to water, stir to dissolve. Wait for about 10 minutes or until foamy. Add lukewarm anise mixture to this. Add persimmon pulp, salt, and 2 cups of whole wheat flour. Beat well. Gradually add the rest of the whole wheat flour and 2½ cups of the bread flour.

Turn out on a well-floured surface and knead for 10 minutes, adding more flour until the dough is smooth and elastic.

Cover with a cloth and let rise for 2 hours or until double in size. Punch down and divide dough into 2 loaves. I shape this bread, and all my persimmon yeast breads, into two long French loaves, put them on to buttered cookie baking sheets, cover and let rise again until doubled (about 1 hour). Bake at 350° for 50 minutes. Let cool and enjoy.

ORANGE ALMOND PERSIMMON BREAD

This is a wonderful holiday bread with a lovely taste of orange. The amount of zest may seem unusual, but it's worth the effort. This bread, like the rest of the persimmon yeast breads, makes delicious toast.

1 c warm water	¾ c sugar
1 c fresh orange juice	¾ c orange zest
1½ T dry yeast	1 c chopped almonds
1 T salt	4 c whole wheat flour
2 c unstrained persimmon pulp	3 to 4 c bread flour

Add 1 tablespoon of the sugar and the yeast to the warm water. Stir to dissolve. Leave until foamy. (About 10 minutes.) Add the orange juice, salt, sugar, persimmon pulp and mix well. Add 2 cups of the whole wheat flour. Beat well. Add the almonds and gradually add the remaining 2 cups of whole-wheat flour and 2½ cups of bread flour. Turn this sticky mess out on to a well-floured surface. Knead for 10 minutes, gradually incorporating the rest of the bread flour, until the dough is smooth and elastic. Cover the bread with a cloth and let rise for two hours or until doubled in size. Punch down and divide into two loaves, place on greased cookie baking sheets and let rise for about an hour or until doubled. Bake at 350° for 50 minutes.

PERSIMMON GINGER BREAD

2 c water
1½ T dry yeast
½ c sugar
2 c persimmon pulp, unstrained
1 T. salt

½ c chopped preserved ginger
7–8 c bread flour
1 c raisins, 1 c chopped pecans
(optional)

Follow the directions on other yeast breads, using the ingredients listed here. You can substitute whole wheat flour for some of the bread flour if you prefer more fiber in your breads. Using all bread flour will produce a loaf with a lovely deep orange color. Adding the raisins and/or nuts always adds interest to your bread – especially for raisin nuts.

PERSIMMON BREAD WITH CINNAMON AND RAISINS

This is the only yeast bread I've included that features strained persimmon pulp. Don't be intimidated by the amount of cinnamon. (But then again, I like cinnamon.) This is definitely a breakfast or tea bread.

2½ T dry yeast dissolved in 1 c water
2 eggs at room temperature
1 c sugar plus 1 T
2 c strained persimmon pulp

4 c whole wheat flour
4 c bread flour
1 T salt
1½ T cinnamon
1 c raisins

In a large mixing bowl, add 1 tablespoon of sugar and the dry yeast to the warm water and stir to dissolve. Leave until foamy and then add the eggs. Mix well and add the sugar, persimmon pulp, salt and cinnamon. Add 2 cups of the whole wheat flour. Beat well. Add the raisins and then all but 1 cup of the flour, beating the dough as well as you can to incorporate the flour. Turn out on a well-floured surface and knead the bread for 10 minutes, gradually adding the rest of the flour, until the dough is smooth and elastic. Cover the bread and let rise until doubled in size. Punch down and shape into 1 large loaf (or 2 smaller ones,) place on greased baking sheets and let rise again for an hour. Bake at 350° for 1 hour.

ONION (YES, ONION...) PERSIMMON BREAD
WITH A SURPRISE

Famed cookbook author Anna Thomas moved to my Ojai neighborhood a few years ago. She asked me if I had a recipe for a persimmon bread that went well with cheese, a bread that was not sweet. This is the recipe I gave her.

2 T butter
2 medium size yellow onions chopped
2 c warm water
1 1/2 T dry yeast
1 T brown sugar
2 c persimmon pulp, unstrained

1½ T garlic salt
1 t ground sage
4 c whole wheat flour
4 c bread flour
1½ c grated mozzarella or jack cheese

Melt butter in a large frying pan. Add chopped onion and, stirring often, sauté until golden over medium heat (about 10 minutes.) Set aside to cool. Meanwhile, in a large mixing bowl add the yeast and sugar to 1 cup of the warm water. Stir to dissolve and set aside to proof. When it's foamy, add remaining water, persimmon pulp, salt, sage and 2 cups of the whole wheat flour. Beat well. Now add the onions and all but one cup of the remaining flour. Turn out on a floured board and knead for 10 minutes, gradually adding the rest of the flour, until the dough is smooth and elastic and stops absorbing flour. Set aside to rise for 2 hours or until doubled in size. Punch down and divide in two. At this point you can shape bread into two loaves, place on greased baking sheets, let rise and bake. OR... you can divide dough in half, and roll out each half into a 12-by-10 inch rectangle. Sprinkle the middle of each rectangle with cheese, roll up, seal the edge with a little water, and place on baking sheets. This is a wonderful treat – excellent with soup on a winter night. I rather enjoy working with yeast dough and a rolling pin, but you can make this bread without this added task if you just want to experiment with the onion sage persimmon combination. Either rolled out or not, bake the loaves for 50 minutes at 350°.

ORANGE PERSIMMON ROLLS

½ c hot water
1½ T dry yeast
½ c sugar
1 egg
¾ c fresh orange juice

¼ c orange zest
1 c of strained persimmon puree (about 3 or 4)
1 T salt
4 c bread flour

In a large mixing bowl, stir yeast and 2 teaspoons of sugar into the hot water until both dissolve. Set aside until bubbly – about 10 minutes. Then add orange juice, persimmon puree, butter, the rest of the sugar, orange zest, salt and 1 cup of the flour. Beat well. Gradually add 2½ cups of the remaining flour. Turn out onto a floured board and knead for 10 minutes, adding the rest of the flour until the dough is smooth and elastic. Add more flour to the board and roll out the dough into an approximately 10-by-15 inch square. Using a glass, cut out rolls. Place these on a well-greased baking sheet. Let rise for about an hour or until doubled and bake at 350° for 20 minutes. You should have about 20 rolls.

PERSIMMON MUFFINS

2 c flour
1 t baking soda
1 t baking powder
½ t salt
½ t cinnamon or ¼ t allspice

1 c persimmon pulp
¼ c vegetable oil
⅓ c honey
2 eggs
½ c raisins and walnuts (optional)

Combine dry ingredients in a large bowl. Combine persimmon pulp, oil, honey and eggs in a food processor or blender and process until mixed well. Add to flour mixture. Stir until flour is just moistened and lump free. Spoon into muffin tins lined with paper. Bake in a 350° oven for 15 to 20 minutes. Makes about 12 muffins.

PERSIMMON CORN MUFFINS

1 c corn meal
1½ c flour
½ c sugar
1 T baking powder
1 t salt
2 eggs
½ c melted butter plus 1 T for onion sauté

1 c persimmon pulp, unstrained
½ c sour cream
1 c corn kernels
1 clove garlic minced
1 onion chopped
1 c grated Cheddar cheese
½ t chili paste

Chop the onion and garlic and sauté in 1 tablespoon of butter over medium heat for 5 minutes or until golden. Set aside to cool a bit. Measure dry ingredients and mix together in a separate bowl (cornmeal, salt, flour, sugar and baking powder). In another mixing bowl, beat eggs and add persimmon pulp, mix well. Add melted butter, sour cream, corn, sautéed onion, cheese and chili paste. Add dry ingredients and mix. Bake in paper-lined muffin tins at 400° for 20 to 25 minutes. Makes about 18 medium sized muffins. These are good to serve with soups or as a side to main course chilies and Mexican stews.

DRIED PERSIMMON NUT BREAD

1 c chopped dried persimmons
2½ T butter
1 t salt
1¼ c boiling water
1 egg

1¼ c sugar
1 t vanilla
2 c bread flour
1 t baking powder
1 t baking soda
¾ cup nuts

Chop the persimmons taking care to check for seeds. Put persimmons, butter and salt into small bowl and pour the boiling water over them. Let cool for 10 minutes. In the meantime, beat egg and add vanilla and sugar. Add the persimmon-water blend. Mix the dry ingredients and add them. Stir well. Add the nuts. Pour into two small well-greased loaf pans or 1 larger. Bake at 350° for about an hour.

HIGH FIBER LOW FAT PERSIMMON NUT BREAD

You can find lots of recipes for persimmon quick breads on the web. This one is not as sweet or high in fat as most, but I think it's still delicious and fun to make as a gift. The recipe yields 2 small loaves.

2 eggs	½ c non-fat milk
1 c persimmon puree	½ c wheat germ
1 c of sugar	2 t cinnamon
½ c canola oil	2 t baking soda
½ c water	1 t baking powder
2 c whole wheat flour	1 t salt
1½ c regular flour	1 c raisins
	½ c chopped walnuts

Beat the eggs in a large bowl. Add the oil, sugar, persimmon and water and mix well. In another mixing bowl sift the flour, combine the dry ingredients and then add them to the persimmon batter. Beat well and then add the raisins and the nuts. Pour into two greased loaf pans and bake in a 350° oven for 50 to 60 minutes or until a toothpick comes out clean. Cool in pans and then enjoy.

SOUPS

SOUPS

PERSIMMON CHICKEN SOUP

1 T garlic	¼ c persimmon pulp, strained
1 onion	1 lime – zest and juice
1 rib celery	1 t Chinese chili paste (or to taste)
1 Anaheim pepper	1 t salt
1 half chicken breast, boned and skinned	1 c fresh or frozen corn kernels
3 cans chicken broth	½ c cilantro
1 8-oz. can tomato sauce	Sour cream (optional)

Mince the garlic and set aside. Chop the onion, celery and pepper. Melt butter or oil in a large soup pot and sauté the onion and garlic for about 7 minutes. Add the celery and pepper and cook for another 2 – 3 minutes. In the mean time, chop chicken and then add to pan. Sauté briefly – until opaque. Add broth, tomato sauce, lime, corn, chili paste and salt. Bring to a low boil, then reduce heat, cover and simmer for 20 minutes. Uncover and add persimmon. Taste and adjust seasonings to taste. Sprinkle each serving with chopped cilantro and a dollop of sour cream. This delicious, colorful soup serves 4 as an entrée and 8 as a side dish. It also freezes well.

ROASTED *FUYU* PERSIMMON SOUP WITH RED MISO PASTE

3 Fuyu persimmons	1½ t salt
1 T corn or canola oil	2 T red miso paste
1 T minced garlic	Zest and juice of 2 limes
1 carrot, peeled and chopped	1 can of garbanzos, drained and rinsed
1 onion, chopped	
3 cans chicken or vegetable broth	Chopped cilantro for garnish

Peel the persimmons. Chop them into quarters and roast them in a 400° oven for 1 hour. Let them cool a bit and then chop them somewhat finer, checking for any hidden seeds. Set aside. In a heavy saucepan, heat the oil and sauté onion and garlic for 10 minutes or until golden. Add the chopped carrot, broth, roasted persimmons, salt, lime, miso and garbanzos. Bring to a low boil, then turn heat down and simmer covered for 25 to 30 minutes. Whirl in a food processor in batches. Return to sauce pan and taste. Adjust seasonings. More salt? More miso? Top each serving of soup with a little chopped cilantro. Serves 6 hungry folk.

THAI PERSIMMON PEANUT SOUP

This one is my attempt at another version of Thai peanut sauce – the delicious concoction Thai restaurants serve up with their satays. It makes for a very satisfying soup.

1-2 onions, chopped
2 stalks celery, chopped
1 Anaheim pepper, chopped
1 T garlic minced
1 T ginger minced
2 T peanut oil
2 chicken thighs, skinned, boned and chopped
5-6 c chicken broth
1 T fish sauce

1 t Chinese chili sauce
1 lime - zest and juice
½ to ¾ c peanut butter (the natural stuff is a better choice)
1 can low-fat coconut milk
½ c strained persimmon pulp
1 c frozen or fresh French cut green beans (pre-steamed if fresh)
1 apple, peeled and chopped
¼ c peanuts, chopped

In a medium sauce pan big enough for a batch of soup, sauté the onion, garlic, ginger, celery and pepper in 1 tablespoon of the oil until the vegetables are limp (about 5 minutes). Remove from the pan and set aside. Add the remaining oil to the pan, heat and sauté the chicken until opaque (about 1 minute.) Then add the chicken broth, peanut butter, fish sauce, chili sauce, and lime. Stir until peanut butter is incorporated, and heat the soup to boiling. Turn down the heat, cover the pan and simmer for 20 minutes. Uncover and add the persimmon, coconut milk and green beans…..simmer a bit longer and then serve. Top each bowl with chopped apple and peanuts if desired. Serves 6.

ANN'S 'SIMMON MINESTRONE

Don't laugh. This version of the Italian favorite is good with or without the persimmon, but naturally I can't help feeling that it gives the soup a special mamamia pizzazz.

2 onions
3 cloves garlic
1 red bell pepper
2 stalks celery
2 carrots
2 T olive oil
½ lb. Italian sausage (the turkey version is fine)
1 8-oz. can of tomato sauce

2 cans garbanzo beans
1 qt chicken broth
Juice and zest of two lemons
2 6-inch sprigs rosemary
½ c persimmon puree
Chopped basil or green onion, for garnish
Salt, to taste
½ c cooked rice or pasta (optional)

Begin by chopping the vegetables. Heat the olive oil in a large soup pan and add the onions and garlic. Sauté for 5 minutes. Remove, add some more olive oil to the pan and brown the sausage, breaking it up into small pieces. Drain off most of the fat. Return all vegetables to the pan. Drain the beans and rinse them, then puree half of them in a food processor with ½ cup of chicken broth and the tomato sauce. Add remaining broth, lemon zest and lemon peel and rosemary to the soup mix and add the garbanzo puree as well. Bring to a boil over medium heat, then cover and simmer for about 40 minutes. Add persimmon puree and remaining garbanzo beans. Taste and adjust seasonings. Serve with chopped fresh basil or green onion on top. Serves 6 to 8.

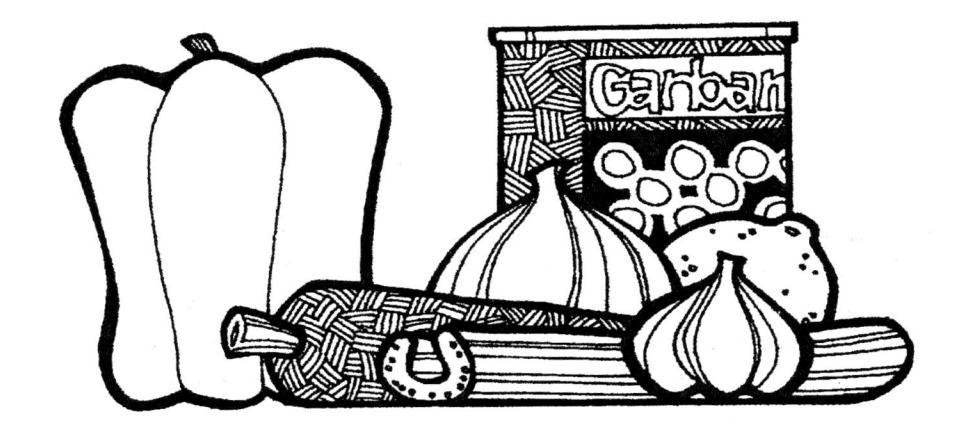

HOT AND MOSTLY SOUR PERSIMMON SOUP WITH TOFU AND MUSHROOMS

This is my version of hot and sour soup. You won't be aware of a sweet flavor . . . just a little bit less sour. The persimmon adds color as well. This soup is a nourishing favorite at our house.

½ c barley
1 onion
1 large portabella mushroom
1½ T canola oil
1 T garlic (about 3 large cloves)
1 T chopped ginger
6 c chicken broth

½ c tomato sauce
¼ c rice vinegar
1 t chili paste
1 c soft tofu
½ c persimmon puree
1 t salt
Chopped cilantro

Cook the barley according to package directions. While the barley is simmering, assemble the soup. Heat the oil in your soup pot and add the onion and mushroom. Cook over medium heat for 5 minutes and then add ginger and garlic and cook for another minute. Add the broth, tomato sauce, vinegar, and chili paste, bring to a boil, then cover, turn down the heat and leave to simmer for 20 minutes. Add cooked barley, persimmon and tofu, adjust seasoning, and serve with chopped cilantro on top. Serves 6.

SWEET MAMA ROASTED PERSIMMON SOUP WITH STAR ANISE

This interesting soup is based on a recipe from Barbara Tropp's book China Moon.

3 *Fuyu* persimmons
1 T corn or canola oil
1 T minced ginger
1½ t minced garlic
1 onion chopped

1 small piece cinnamon bark (2 inches or so)
1 star anise
3 cans chicken or vegetable broth
Salt and pepper to taste

See instructions for roasting persimmons in the introduction to this book, or use a stash of previously roasted persimmons. Heat the oil in a heavy sauce and stir-fry the garlic and ginger for 15 seconds. Add the onion and sauté over medium to low heat for 10 minutes or until golden. Add the stock, the persimmons, star anise, and cinnamon bark. Cover and simmer for 30 minutes. Remove bark and star anise and then puree the soup in batches in a food processor. Return to pot; add salt and pepper. Taste and adjust seasoning. Serves 6.

ROASTED PERSIMMON SOUP WITH LEMON GRASS AND WHITE BEANS

1 T corn or canola oil
1½ t garlic minced
1 T ginger minced
1 small jalapeno minced
1 T lemon grass minced
1 onion chopped
1 carrot chopped

3 cans chicken broth
2 limes – zest and juice
1½ c roasted *Fuyu* persimmon
1 can coconut milk
1 can small white beans, drained and rinsed
Cilantro for garnish

Follow directions for preceding roasted persimmon soups, but this time add minced jalapeno and lemon grass to the garlic, ginger sauté. The white beans add a rich texture to this version of roasted persimmon soup.
Serves 6.

ROASTED PERSIMMON BLACK BEAN SOUP WITH CUMIN

3 *Fuyu* persimmons
1 T corn or canola oil
1 T minced garlic
½ jalapeno, minced
2 onions, chopped
1 stalk celery, chopped
1 carrot, chopped

3 cans beef broth
1 can tomato sauce
2 lemons, zest and juice
1 T cumin
1 can black beans
1 c chopped ham
Salt and pepper to taste
Sour cream

Follow directions in preceding recipes for roasted *Fuyu* soup. Coarsely chop both fruit and vegetables. Heat oil in large sauce pan and briefly sauté garlic and jalapeno. Add broth, persimmons, vegetables, tomato sauce, lemon, beans and cumin. Bring to a low boil, turn heat down, cover and simmer for

30 minutes. Whirl in a blender, a couple of cups at a time, and return to soup pot. Add ham and a little salt and pepper. Heat gently and serve with a little sour cream on top. Serves 6.

MAINLINING VITAMIN A CURRIED CARROT AND PERSIMMON SOUP

6 carrots
2-3 stalks celery
1 onion
1 T ginger
1 t garlic
1 T canola oil
2 heaping t curry powder

1 t salt
2 T lemon juice and the zest from the lemon
1 qt chicken broth
1 cinnamon stick
½ c persimmon puree
1 can coconut milk

Peel the carrots and chop them. Mince the garlic and ginger and chop the onions and celery. Sauté the vegetables for about 10 minutes on low to medium heat. Add the curry powder and salt. Working in batches, puree the vegetables with a cup or two of the chicken broth in a food processor. Return to pot and add the rest of the chicken broth and cinnamon stick. Bring to a low boil, turn the heat down, cover and simmer the soup for about 30 minutes. Add persimmon, coconut milk and lemon juice and heat gently. Serve with chopped green onion or cilantro as a garnish.

CHILLED PERSIMMON SOUP WITH PINEAPPLE AND RUM

This soup makes a refreshing first course for a summer lunch or dinner.

2 star anise
1 c strained persimmon puree
1 can low fat coconut milk
1 6 oz can pineapple juice

1 or 2 T lime juice
2 T honey
2 T dark rum

In a small saucepan, heat 1 cup of water until boiling. Drop in the two star anise and turn heat off. Leave to steep. Whirl persimmon pulp in a food processor with the lime juice, honey and rum. Pour into medium size bowl and add juice, coconut milk and rum. Now add the star anise and chill for several hours. Top each serving with a little chopped cilantro.

COLD PERSIMMON BISQUE WITH ORANGE JUICE AND CINNAMON

Another cold soup for hot summer days. Very pretty with the sliced strawberries floating on each serving. And it's easy to make as well.

2 c buttermilk
2 T honey
½ t cinnamon

1 c persimmon puree
1 c fresh orange juice
½ c sliced strawberries

Whirl the buttermilk, honey and cinnamon in a food processor until smooth. In a separate mixing bowl, add the persimmon and orange juice and stir until well blended. Chill for at least 4 hours. Serve with sliced strawberries on top. Serves about 8 as a first course . . . or a unique dessert.

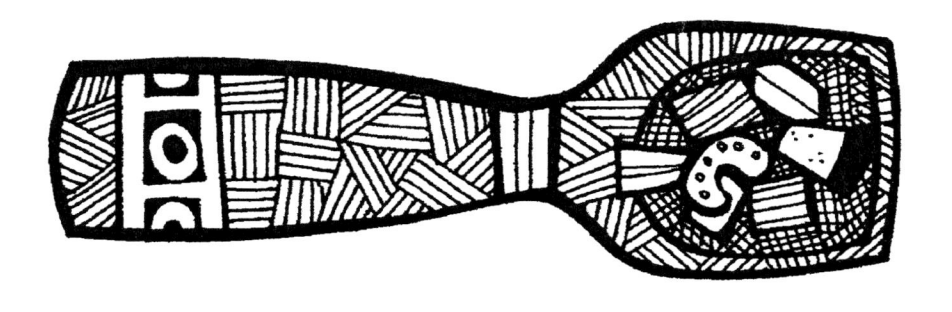

SALADS & SALAD DRESSINGS

SALADS AND SALAD DRESSINGS

PERSIMMON, JICAMA AND CUCUMBER SALAD

This recipe is adapted from Susanna Foo's Chinese Cuisine. I've served this as my offering at a Thanksgiving potluck.

1 c peeled cucumber
1 T coarse salt
1 c jicama cut into ½-inch cubes
¼ c minced red onion
2 c cold water
1 medium *Fuyu* persimmon, ripe but firm, peeled and diced

½ jalapeno pepper, seeded and diced or pinch dried red pepper flakes
2 T orange juice
2 T rice wine vinegar
¼ c olive oil
Salt and pepper to taste

Cut the cucumber into ½ inch dice and mix with the salt. Let stand for 10 minutes and then rinse and drain. Soak the onion in the water for 2 minutes and then drain. In a medium bowl, mix the cucumber, jicama, onion, jalapeno pepper. Add the persimmon. In a small bowl, mix the orange juice, vinegar, olive oil and a little salt. Add to salad. Taste and adjust seasonings. This salad serves 6 to 8 and makes a colorful, crunchy side dish.

TURKEY AND PERSIMMON SALAD

This is an easy make-ahead salad that can be used for left-over turkey. It serves 4 to 6 and makes a nice addition to a picnic.

⅓ c mayonnaise
¼ c plain yogurt
1 T curry powder
2 c diced cooked turkey
1½ c diced *Fuyu* persimmon

¼ c chopped red onion
½ c roasted peanuts or pecans
1 c diced celery
1 c chopped crisp green apple

Whisk curry powder, mayonnaise, and yogurt together in a medium bowl. Add salt and pepper to taste. Set aside. You can make this a day earlier if you wish but cover and refrigerate. To assemble salad, mix turkey, onion, nuts, celery and apple in a large bowl. Add persimmon and dressing and toss well. Taste and adjust seasoning. Feel free to add or subtract ingredient amounts according to what you like or have on hand. No left-over turkey? Leave it out. The persimmon, apple, celery, nut combination works fine by itself.

MIXED GREEN SALAD WITH *FUYU* PERSIMMON AND RASPBERRY PERSIMMON VINAIGRETTE

Inspired by a recipe using mangos in Deborah Madison's book The Savory Way, *this colorful salad features persimmons two ways – Fuyus sliced and served with avocados and bananas on top of fresh greens, topped with the Hachiya and raspberry vinaigrette. It's a colorful and memorable dish, served either as the main attraction at an autumn lunch or as the first course at a special dinner. Serves 6.*

2 shallots, finely diced
2 limes, zest and juice
¼ c light olive oil
4 T persimmon puree
½ c raspberries
2 T balsamic vinegar

1 large ripe but firm avocado
1 large ripe but firm *Fuyu* persimmon
1 slightly green banana
½ c pecans
1½ heads butter and red lettuce mixed

First make the dressing. Put the raspberries in a strainer and position the strainer over a small bowl. Press the berries with your fingers and squeeze the raspberry juice into this bowl. Discard the mashed berries (or eat them). Add the shallots, limes, olive oil, persimmon puree, a little salt and the balsamic vinegar, whisk it all and taste. You may want to add more vinegar. Put aside. (The dressing may be made up to 24 hours before serving.) Roast the pecans in a 325° oven for 15 minutes. Just before serving, distribute mixed lettuce greens on 6 plates, place sliced persimmon, avocado, and banana slices on them, and sprinkle with pecans. Spoon vinaigrette over each serving and wait for the smiles from your guests.

ROASTED DRIED PERSIMMON SALAD WITH GOAT CHEESE

This recipe is adapted from one featuring dried figs. I found it in the Los Angeles Times a couple of years ago. I used to find the Times food pages a creative, challenging source of great ideas, but lately it's morphed to a mere source of up-scale restaurant reviews. Oh well. I served this at a pot-luck to enthusiastic reviews.

Balsamic Vinaigrette
1 small shallot, finely minced
3 T balsamic vinegar
½ t minced fresh rosemary

1½ t Dijon mustard
½ c olive oil
½ t salt

Whisk all the above together and taste. Adjust seasonings.

SALAD

8 dried persimmons, chopped and seeded (about 1 cup)
2 T brown sugar
1 small shallot, finely minced
½ T minced rosemary

½ c port
1 c pecans or walnuts
8 c mixed salad greens
½ c crumbled goat cheese

Heat the oven to 375°. Combine the persimmons, brown sugar, shallots, rosemary, balsamic vinegar and port in a glass baking dish. Bake, stirring a few times, for about 30 minutes. Cool. While the persimmons are toasting, toast the nuts on a dry baking sheet 5 to 7 minutes. Set aside to cool. Wash and dry the greens, place on 8 salad plates. Sprinkle with roasted persimmons. Drizzle each plate with a tablespoon or so of dressing, then add some nuts and goat cheese. Alternatively, assemble the salad in a large bowl.

PERSIMMON FRUIT SALAD WITH TAMARIND

The tamarind and chili add an interesting bite to this one.

1½ t tamarind concentrate
2 T hot water
2 T packed brown sugar
1 small chili pepper, halved and seeded or ½ t Chinese chili paste
2 T peanuts
1 t salt

½ cucumber, peeled, seeded and chopped
2 *Fuyu* persimmons, peeled, seeded and chopped
1 *Fuji* apple, seeded and chopped
1 Asian pear, seeded and chopped

Whirl the tamarind, water, sugar, peanuts and salt in a food processor. Toss the fruit in a large bowl, add the dressing and serve. Serves 4 as a small side salad.

ROASTED *FUYU* PERSIMMON SALAD WITH CUMIN AND LIME

This is a unique, appealing salad with an intriguing mix of flavors. I have a hard time saving any for guests when I make it. I based this one on a roasted sweet potato recipe I got off the net. My husband Jim suggested the garlic and it's an interesting addition. Of course the garlic smells wonderful while roasting.

5-6 large *Fuyu* persimmons, peeled and chopped into ½ inch wedges.
6 garlic cloves, peeled
¼ c olive oil
1 t salt

1 t ground cumin
2 scallions, both white and green, chopped
2 T lime juice or more to taste
¼ c chopped cilantro

Put the persim2mons and garlic in a large roasting pan that has been lined with aluminum foil. Sprinkle with salt. In a small bowl whisk together oil, salt, and cumin and brush the persimmons and garlic with some of it – saving most for the dressing. Roast the persimmons in a 350° oven for about an hour.

Remove from oven and cool. Put persimmons in your serving bowl. Chop scallions and sprinkle over fruit. Chop roasted garlic and add. Whisk lime juice into remaining cumin oil with salt and pepper to taste and drizzle over salad. Add cilantro and serve. Leftovers will keep in the refrigerator for a day or two. Serves 4 to 6 as a side salad.

ROASTED *FUYU* PERSIMMON POTATO SALAD WITH LEMON AND ROSEMARY

This is another roasted Fuyu persimmon salad. The colors are striking. I love the rosemary lemon combination, but go easy if you're not a rosemary fan.

3-4 *Fuyu* persimmons
3 medium red or gold potatoes, skinned
3 green onions, both white and green, chopped
Zest of 1 lemon

2 t to 1 T chopped fresh rosemary, or to taste
2 T olive oil
1 T lemon juice
Salt to taste

Peel 3 firm *Fuyu* persimmons and slice them about ½ inch thick. Line a baking sheet with aluminum foil and spray it with cooking spray. Spread the persimmons on it and spray them with a little of the spray, too. Roast them at 400° for about an hour, flipping them midway. Remove from oven and let cool. In the meantime, wash and chop the potatoes into 1 inch dice, and steam them for about 5 minutes – or done to your taste. (I like my potatoes firm.) When the potatoes are done, add them to the persimmons in a medium sized serving bowl. Add the rosemary and lemon zest. Whisk the olive oil and lemon juice together and add this to the vegetables and fruit. Add the chopped green onion and salt to taste. Serve at room temperature. Serves 4 to 6.

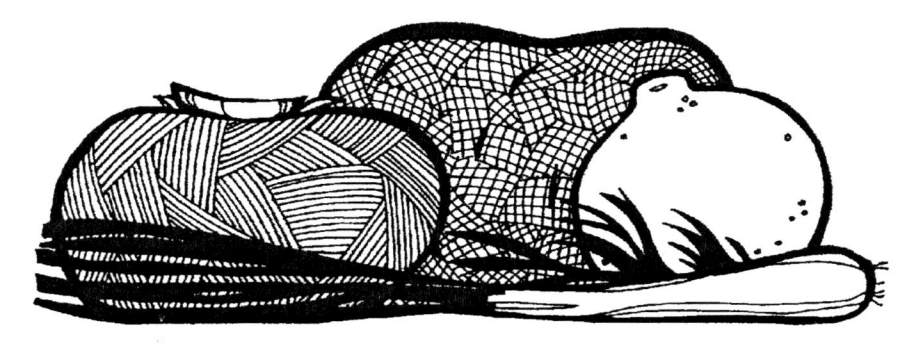

ROASTED PERSIMMON SALAD
WITH ROASTED CARROTS AND CINNAMON

Yes, another roasted persimmon salad. I love to experiment with them. If you like cinnamon, give this one a try.

6 large *Fuyu* persimmons, peeled, sliced and roasted
6 carrots, peeled, sliced in half and roasted
4 green onions, chopped
4 stalks celery, chopped fine

3-4 T goat cheese, crumbled
1 lime - zest and juice
2 to 3 T olive oil
1 t cinnamon (or more to taste)
½ t salt

Roast the persimmons as directed in previous recipes. At the same time, roast the carrots, peeled and sliced in half. Let them cool after roasting and then cut carrots into smaller pieces. Chop the other vegetables, whisk the lime juice, oil and cinnamon together, and mix everything together in a medium bowl. Serves 4 to 6 as a side salad.

STILL ANOTHER ROASTED PERSIMMON SALAD...
THIS ONE WITH CAULIFLOWER

I seem to be a relatively solitary fan of cauliflower. Many of my friends don't care for it. Try this version and you may become a convert. The secret is to steam the cut-up vegetable for just a minute or two, not the five or even ten minutes suggested by all too many cookbooks.

3 *Fuyu* persimmons
3-4 green onions

1 head of cauliflower

MUSTARD VINAIGRETTE

1 egg
1 t Dijon mustard
1 clove garlic, peeled and chopped

3 T white wine vinegar
7 T olive oil
½ t salt

Follow the directions in previous recipes for roasting the persimmons. Prepare the dressing (whirl in a blender) and set aside. Cut the cauliflower into small bite sized pieces and steam them 1 to 2 minutes. Set aside in a medium size serving bowl and let cool. Chop the persimmons and add them to the cauliflower. Just before serving, chop the green onions and add them. Pour dressing over and toss. Adjust seasoning and serve warm or at room temperature. Serves 4 to 6.

BRAISED RED CABBAGE, ONION AND PERSIMMON SALAD

This has become one of my favorite summer lunch dishes. I often make it using frozen roasted Fuyus.

1 onion chopped
1 half of a red cabbage
1 T canola oil
Juice and zest of an orange
3-4 T balsamic vinegar

1 c fresh or roasted Fuyu persimmon, chopped
½ c feta cheese, crumbled
1 apple, chopped and ½ c pecans (optional)

Heat the oil in a medium sized sauce pan and sauté the onion over medium heat for about 5 minutes. In the mean time, core and chop the cabbage. Add cabbage, orange juice and zest and vinegar to the pan. Cover and simmer for about 20 minutes. Uncover and add persimmon and cheese (and apples and nuts if you're using them). Serve either warm or at room temperature. If refrigerated, this salad keeps for about 4 days, if you're using roasted persimmon. Otherwise, serve immediately. Serves 4.

FRESH *FUYU* PERSIMMON, AVOCADO AND SPINACH SALAD

This one was given to me by my good friend Dixie Adeniran. It's based on a recipe from Gourmet magazine. The original called for watercress, but I prefer spinach. Both are good.

2 T lemon juice
4 t water
1½ T sweet white miso paste
¼ t black pepper
⅛ t salt
⅓ c olive oil

3 firm ripe avocados
3 firm ripe *Fuyu* persimmons, peeled, seeded and thinly sliced
8 c spinach

Blend together lemon juice, water, miso, pepper and salt until smooth. With the motor running, add oil in a slow stream in 3 batches, blending until emulsified. Season with salt and pepper. Pit and peel the avocados, then cut into thin slices. Gently toss together the persimmon, avocados and 6 T of the dressing. Toss spinach with just enough dressing to coat (about 3 tablespoons) in another bowl. Divide persimmon mixture among 6 plates and top with spinach. Serve.

DRIED PERSIMMON, ORANGE AND FENNEL SALAD WITH POMEGRANATES AND ANISE

Here's another example of my delight in anise-flavored cooking. The dried persimmons you use for this must be ones you have not stored in the freezer, but persimmons dry enough to have natural sugar crystals, dry persimmons that have hardened. Otherwise, they will not stand up to the stove simmering process with anise and orange. This gives them a wonderful taste that I find addictive. And I always make more than I need for the salad so that I can eat them out of hand.

2 dried persimmons, quartered
¾ c fresh orange juice
Zest of one orange
1 t anise
1 t mustard
2 T rice vinegar
3 T canola oil
Salt to taste
2 T chopped red onion
½ fennel bulb, chopped
6 c bronze lettuce
3 leaves Chinese or napa cabbage, chopped
Seeds of one pomegranate

Combine first three ingredients in a small sauce pan. Bring to a boil and reduce heat. Simmer until fruit has softened and juice is reduced to about 3 tablespoons (about 5 minutes). Cool the fruit and then chop it. Set aside. Combine the persimmon orange simmered juice, rice vinegar, canola oil and mustard, whisk to blend. Season to taste with salt. Combine lettuce and cabbage. Divide among 4 plates. Sprinkle with red onion, chopped fennel and pomegranate seeds. Spoon dressing over all and top with chopped 'simmons. Serves 4.

OJAI WALDORF SALAD WITH FRESH *FUYU*

This one is courtesy of my good friend Sally Hoover, who had this published (minus the Fuyu persimmon) in Sunset magazine several years ago. We both agree it's even better with my favorite fruit added. Sally notes that chopped dried persimmons are another possible addition.

1 large Granny Smith or Pippin apple or other crisp fairly tart apple
1 *Fuyu* persiimon, also crisp
1 jicama of same size as apple
½ c golden raisins
¼ c dates, cut into pieces
½ t crystallized ginger to taste

½ t grated orange rind plus juice of orange
⅛ t each (or more to taste) freshly grated nutmeg and cinnamon
¼ c mayonnaise mixed with
¼ c plain yogurt
½ c peanuts

Grate orange rind and then squeeze juice into mixing bowl. Add peeled apple, jicama and persimmon cut into bite-sized pieces. Add spices, raisins, dates and ginger. Dress with equal parts mayonnaise and yogurt or less of one or other to suit your taste. Stir and chill for a couple of hours before serving. Add peanuts just before serving. Sprinkle them on top and mix lightly. The peanuts will lose their crunchy texture fairly quickly.

PERSIMMON YOGURT MOLDED SALAD

Molded salads have fallen out of foodie favor and are regarded with distaste and hauteur by many cooks. But my nephew Kenny Baxter loves them, so this one is for Kenny. Besides, it's very pretty and has an unexpected crunch with the pomegranates. And more importantly, it tastes good.

1¼ c water
1 package orange-flavored gelatin
1 t lemon zest
2 T lemon juice

Dash of salt
1 c strained persimmon pulp
2 c unflavored yogurt
Seeds of 1 pomegranate

Pour water into a medium sized saucepan. Place pan over medium heat, add orange gelatin and bring to simmering, stirring until gelatin is dissolved (about

2 minutes). Remove from heat and stir in lemon peel, juice, and salt. Cool, and then add yogurt and persimmon pulp. Blend with a wire whip, add pomegranate seeds and pour into mold or bowl. Cover and chill until firm. That takes about 3 hours. Serves 6.

MOLDED PERSIMMON SALAD WITH COTTAGE CHEESE, GINGER AND OTHER WEIRD THINGS

Kenny Baxter got me started on molded salads but my friend Lynn Lykins spurred my interest and enthusiasm. Her grandmother specialized in them. Lynn has reminded me that they can be very refreshing on hot California summer days. So, during the summer, go to the freezer and fetch your persimmon pulp for this interesting version of a Jello salad. It packs a protein punch with the cottage cheese. And your friends and family will never guess that something so good for them is included in the ingredients. Add more chopped vegetables if you want more crunch. The raw onion adds punch to the mix.

1 package plain gelatin
½ package (6 ounces) orange Jello
1 c water
1 t (or a little bit more) minced ginger
Pinch red chili flakes
2 c low-fat cottage cheese

1 c persimmon pulp, strained
½ c fresh orange juice
1 T rice vinegar
1-2 carrots grated
1 stalk celery, chopped
½ onion sliced, soaked for 2 minutes in cold water and then drained and diced.

Add the water to a small sauce pan and sprinkle the plain gelatin over it. Leave to soften for two minutes and then heat to boiling. Remove from heat and add *Jello*, ginger and chili flakes. Stir for two minutes or until fully dissolved. Set aside. Prepare vegetables and set aside. Puree cottage cheese and persimmon pulp in a food processor. Add vinegar and orange juice and pour into a medium serving dish. Add *Jello* mixture and vegetables and stir to blend. At this point either pour into mold or leave in bowl. Refrigerate for 3 to 4 hours before serving. This dish will keep for up to 4 days. Serves 6 to 8 as a side dish.

APPLE PERSIMMON MOLDED SALAD

Another candidate in the molded salad derby. I came up with this one because I have 2 apple trees. And a lot of apples. And the pureed cottage cheese persimmon mix is an interesting combination.

1 package plain gelatin
½ c water
1 c apple juice
1 c strained persimmon pulp
1 t cinnamon
1 pint cottage cheese
1 T lemon juice

1 T honey
¼ t salt
2 apples (Fujis or Granny Smith), peeled and chopped
1 stalk celery
½ c chopped pecans

Sprinkle the gelatin into the water, let stand for 2 minutes, then heat to boiling. Remove from heat and add apple juice, lemon juice, honey, and cinnamon. Set aside. Whirl cottage cheese and persimmon puree in a food processor until smooth. Mix all together in a medium side bowl . . . at the last adding apples, celery and nuts. Use this bowl for serving or pour into a mold. Chill several hours. Serves 6 to 8.

All of the following dressings are good on mixed green salads and each boasts the lovely orange hue that persimmons provide.

PERSIMMON MAYONNAISE WITH ORANGE

1 egg
2 T strained persimmon pulp
2 T orange juice
2 T rice vinegar

1 t Dijon mustard
4 T canola oil
¼ t Chinese chili paste
Salt to taste

Whirl in a food processor and refrigerate. Keeps for about a week and can be easily doubled.

PERSIMMON MISO MAYONNAISE

1 egg
3 T strained persimmon puree
4 T rice vinegar

½ c canola oil
¾ c red miso paste

Whirl in a food processor and refrigerate. Also keeps for a week.

PERSIMMON SOY CITRUS DRESSING

1 clove garlic minced
2 T ginger minced
Zest and juice of 1 lime
3 T persimmon puree (strained)
3 T orange juice

2 T soy sauce
1 T brown sugar
¼ c canola oil
½ t Chinese chili paste
¼ t salt

Whirl in a blender. Serve on mixed greens with jicama and avocado slices. A zesty vinaigrette.

PINEAPPLE PERSIMMON VINAIGRETTE

A variation of the raspberry persimmon dressing that was used in the recipe for Mixed Green Salad with Fuyu Persimmon.

1 shallot, minced
4 T light olive oil
2 T rice vinegar

2-3 T pineapple juice
3 T persimmon puree
½ t salt

SAUCES, SALSAS, CHUTNEYS & JAMS

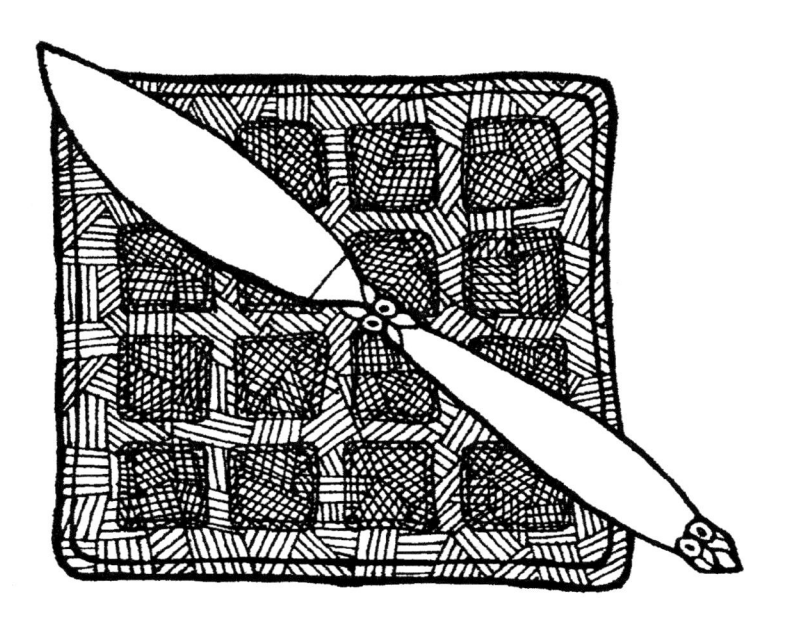

SAUCES, SALSAS, CHUTNEYS AND JAMS

PERSIMMON MISO SAUCE

1 shallot, minced
2 t minced ginger
¼ c canola oil
½ c white wine

4 T strained persimmon pulp
¼ c fresh orange juice
1½ T white miso paste

In a skillet over moderate heat, sauté the shallot and ginger in 1 tablespoon of the oil. Add the wine and reduce by half (about 4 minutes at same moderate heat). Add orange juice and simmer, stirring occasionally for 5 minutes. Stir in the miso, turn off the heat and add the persimmon. Pour in a blender and puree until smooth. With the motor running add the remaining oil. This sauce can be made ahead and refrigerated. Reheat gently before serving over fish or vegetables. Very, very pretty served on top of salmon. And it's delicious.

PERSIMMON TAMARIND SAUCE

2 cloves garlic, minced
1 T minced ginger
3 green onions, white parts (save top
part for garnish)
1 T canola oil
1½ t tamarind concentrate

¼ c chicken broth
3 T strained persimmon puree
1 T honey
1 t salt
2 t cornstarch

Combine garlic, ginger and onion in a small bowl. Mix tamarind, broth, honey, salt and cornstarch in another bowl. Set aside. Heat the oil in a medium sized skillet and sauté garlic mix briefly – about 15 to 20 seconds. Add tamarind sauce ingredients and heat until thickened, then add the persimmon. Serve on steamed vegetables (especially carrots or cauliflower) or fish. This sauce will keep refrigerated for about a week. The tamarind gives it a unique tangy flavor.

FUYU PERSIMMON CHUTNEY

¾ c cider vinegar
1 c chopped onion
1 large green apple, chopped
1 c raisins
1 c sugar
¼ c lemon juice
1 jalapeno pepper, seeded and minced

1 T minced ginger
1 T lemon zest
1 t ground coriander
⅛ t cloves
2½ c chopped peeled *Fuyu* persimmons (2 or 3 large)

For about 3 cups of refrigerated chutney, combine all ingredients (except persimmons) in a heavy saucepan. Bring to a boil over medium heat – stirring occasionally. Reduce heat to medium low and simmer until mixture thickens, about 20 minutes. Add the persimmons and simmer until they are tender, about 5 minutes. Remove from heat and ladle into jars. This chutney keeps for about a week in the refrigerator. Alternatively, double the recipe and process jars in boiling water for 10 minutes.

SUNSET'S APRICOT PERSIMMON CHUTNEY
FOR EITHER *HACHIYA* OR *FUYU* 'SIMMONS

2 lbs ripe *Fuyus* (6 to 7 medium) or 2 lbs soft *Hachiya* (4) persimmons
3½ c water
2 c dried apricots
1½ c raisins

2 T minced fresh ginger
1 T mustard seed
¾ t red chili flakes
1½ c white wine vinegar
1½ c packed brown sugar

For *Fuyu* persimmons – cut off stems and peel off skin. Chop fruit, watching for seeds. You will need 4½ cups of fruit. For *Hachiya* persimmons – pull off stems, then cut fruit in half and scoop pulp out with a spoon. You need 2½ cups of fruit. Once you've finished this, set fruit aside.

If using *Fuyu* persimmons, in a large pan combine fruit with water, apricots, raisins, ginger, mustard seed, and chili. Bring to a boil, reduce heat to a simmer, then cover and cook 10 minutes. Add vinegar and sugar. Simmer uncovered, stirring occasionally, then more frequently as mixture thickens, until most of the liquid evaporates and chutney is reduced to 7 cups, about 45 minutes. Remove from heat.

If using *Hachiya* persimmons, in your large pot, bring water, apricots, raisins, ginger, mustard and chili to boil, then reduce heat to simmer, cover and cook 10 minutes. Add vinegar and sugar, and simmer, uncovered, stirring occasionally until reduced to about 4½ cups, approximately 50 minutes. Stir in *Hachiya* fruit and remove from heat at once.

Salt chutney to taste. Serve warm or store covered in the refrigerator for up to a month, or freeze in small plastic units. You may can the *Fuyu* chutney, but may not do so with the *Hachiya*...heating makes it astringent. Yield for these amounts . . . about 3 pints.

CRANBERRY PERSIMMON RELISH

This recipe came to me from my friend Patty Lunetta, a sister librarian and enthusiastic cook. Given a whole lot of Thanksgiving persimmons, she adapted a favorite cranberry dish, and we can all give thanks!

1 small orange	¼ t cinnamon
1 pound raw cranberries	⅛ t allspice
⅓ c sugar (possibly more to taste.)	¼ t finely grated raw ginger root
¾ c pureed persimmon pulp	Dollop of sour cream (optional garnish)

Begin by cutting the orange into quarters, and then cut each quarter in half and remove the seeds. Place in a food processor along with the cranberries and process until well ground. Put this mixture into a medium size bowl and add the sugar and the persimmon puree and mix well. Add the remaining ingredients, mix well and taste. If you think it needs more sugar, add it. Cover and chill for at least 4 hours.

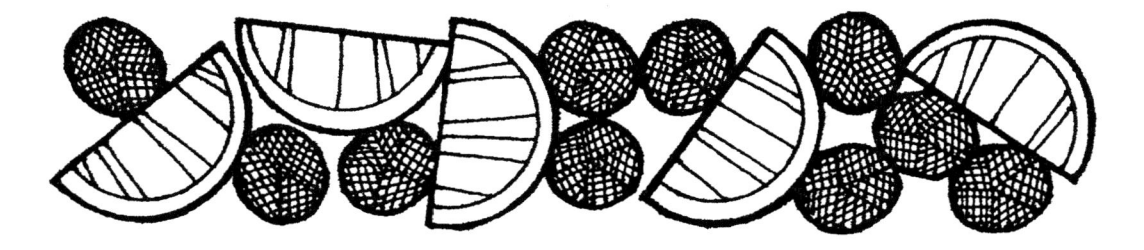

FUYU SALSA

2 serrano chiles
2 T finely minced ginger
¼ c minced green onion
¼ c chopped cilantro

2 c chopped *Fuyu* (2 to 3)
3 T lime juice
2 T brown sugar

Combine all in a bowl and serve along side grilled chicken, fish or vegetables.

PERSIMMON SALSA NO. 2

I got this one off the net. Try serving atop smoked fish on crackers.

4 small or 3 medium size firm *Fuyu* persimmons, peeled and cut into ½ inch cubes
2 T minced shallots
1 T plus 1 t Meyer lemon juice

1 T minced fresh basil
2 t minced seeded jalapeno
2 t minced fresh mint
1 t minced peeled fresh ginger

Mix persimmons, shallots, lemon juice, basil, jalapeno, mint and ginger in a small bowl. Season to taste with salt and pepper. This can be made 4 to 6 hours ahead. Cover and refrigerate but bring to room temperature before serving.

PERSIMMON FREEZER JAM

4 c persimmon puree
3 c sugar

2 T lemon juice
½ t lemon zest

In a large pan, combine persimmon puree and sugar, cook very gently over low heat, stirring until thickened, about 20 minutes. Do not boil. Remove from heat and stir in lemon juice and zest. Pour into sterilized jars and store in refrigerator for up to 2 months or in freezer for up to a year. Makes 2 pints.

DESSERTS

DESSERTS

CHOCOLATE PERSIMMON CAKE with ORANGE ZEST

2½ c regular all purpose flour, unsifted
½ c baker's cocoa
2½ t baking powder
1½ t baking soda
1 t salt
1 c butter (2 sticks), melted

2 c sugar
2 c persimmon pulp, unstrained, about 4
3 eggs
½ c orange zest
1 c chopped nuts

Heat the oven to 350°. Butter a 12-cup Bundt pan with a tablespoon or so of the butter and dust with flour. Knock off the excess and set aside. In a medium-sized bowl mix the flour, baking soda and powder, salt and the cocoa. Set aside. In a large mixing bowl, beat the eggs, add the butter and sugar and beat well. Now add the persimmon puree. Beat again. Now add the dry ingredients, beating for a minute or so, until the batter is smooth. Last, add the nuts and pour the batter into the Bundt pan. Bake for about an hour or until a tester comes out clean. Cool for 10 minutes and then knock on the counter a time or two to loosen. Unmold on your serving plate and cool. Ice with your favorite icing. I prefer the following old standby.

CREAM CHEESE ICING

3 ozs soft cream cheese
1½ T fresh orange juice

6 T soft margarine or butter
2 to 2½ c confectioners' sugar, sifted

Whirl in a food processor until smooth and pour over cake.

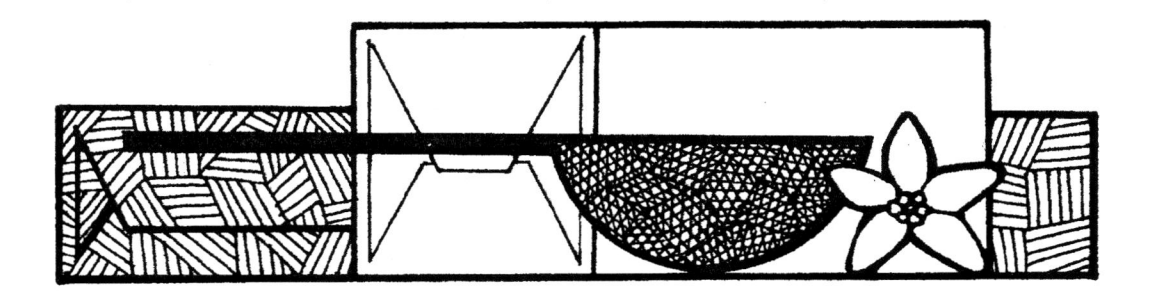

PERSIMMON CARROT CAKE

A new twist on an old favorite and probably my favorite cake of all.

2 c flour	2 eggs
2 t baking soda	1 c strained persimmon
2 t baking powder	1 t vanilla
1 t salt	3 c shredded carrots
2 t cinnamon	¾ c chopped nuts
1½ c sugar	1 T orange zest
1½ c oil	½ c raisins

Sift together all the dry ingredients. Set aside. In a large bowl, beat the eggs and the oil, then add the sugar, persimmon, orange zest and vanilla. Add the flour mixture and finally the carrots, nuts and raisins. Grease a 10-inch Bundt pan, dust it with flour. Add the batter and bake in a 350° oven for 50 to 60 minutes. Let cool and then frost with a basic cream cheese frosting. This great cake will serve up to 20 people.

PERSIMMON CAKE WITH RUM ORANGE ICING

A wonderful cake from the Los Angeles Times.

1 c butter, melted	1¾ t baking soda
1 c dried currants	1 t salt
3 c sifted unbleached flour	1¾ c pureed unpeeled persimmon
1¾ c sugar	4 eggs
1 T ground ginger	½ c dark rum

Butter a 12-cup Bundt pan and dust with flour. Beat the eggs in a large mixing bowl. Add the melted butter, persimmon puree, sugar and rum. Add salt, baking soda and ginger to the flour, then add to batter – mixing well. Last, add the currants and nuts – folding them in with a rubber spatula until thoroughly mixed. Pour the batter into the Bundt pan and bake for 60 to 65 minutes or until a toothpick comes out clean. Cool the cake in the pan for 15 minutes, then knock the pan against the counter a few times to loosen the cake. Unmold onto your serving plate.

RUM ORANGE ICING

3⅔ c confectioners' sugar
¼ c butter, softened
4-5 T orange juice

2 T rum
Zest of one large orange

Whisk the sugar, butter, 3½ tablespoons of the orange juice and rum together until smooth. Add the zest. If the icing is too thick, add ½ tablespoon of orange juice. Pour over your cake.

PERSIMMON ANISE CAKE

My interest in the persimmon anise interface led me to try this combination. The use of the Pernod was inspired by the brandy that appeared in a favorite apple cake recipe. I think it gives this dark, moist cake a lovely kick.

1½ c vegetable oil
2 c sugar
3 eggs
1½ c all purpose flour, sifted
1 T anise seeds
1 t baking soda
1 t salt

1 c whole-wheat flour, sifted
1 c walnuts or pecans, chopped
1 T orange zest . . . or more to taste
1½ c mashed persimmons, unstrained
2 T Pernod

Preheat oven to 350°. In a large bowl, beat oil and sugar until thick. Add eggs and beat well. Add the mashed persimmons. Sift together both flours, baking soda and salt. Add this mixture to your batter and mix. Last, add pernod, orange zest, and nuts. Pour batter into greased and floured Bundt cake pan and bake for 1 hour and 10 minutes, or until a cake tester comes out clean. Let cool for 10 minutes and then unmold. Frost with your favorite frosting or one of the ones I've included. Serves 10 to 12 easily.

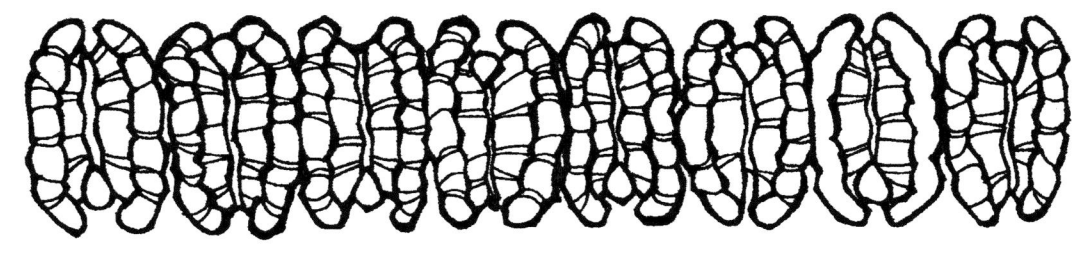

FUYU BUNDT CAKE

My friend Susan Dykstra found this recipe for me. It was originally published in Sunset *some years ago.*

2 t baking soda	2 c flour
3 c chopped firm Fuyus (2 large or 3 small)	1 t baking soda
	1 t salt
½ c butter (1 stick), softened	1 t cinnamon
1⅔ c sugar	½ t ground cloves
2 eggs	½ t nutmeg
2 t lemon juice	1 c walnuts, chopped
2 t vanilla	¾ c raisins

Grease and flour a Bundt cake pan. Preheat oven to 350°. Stir the baking soda into the chopped Fuyus. Set aside. In a large bowl, beat the butter and sugar, add the eggs, lemon juice, vanilla and beat until fluffy. Stir in mix. Sift together the flour, baking powder, salt, cinnamon, cloves and nutmeg. Stir flour into *Fuyu* mixture until blended. Add the nuts and raisins. Pour into Bundt pan. Bake for about 60 minutes or until a toothpick tests clean. Cool in pan for about 15 minutes and then turn onto rack or serving plate. Top with your favorite frosting or one of the previous frosting recipes.

PERSIMMON APPLE STREUSEL CAKE

Several steps, but an interesting, delicious cake that keeps well.

APPLES

3 T butter	3 T sugar
4 c chopped crisp apples (about 4)	1 t cinnamon

Melt butter in a large skillet over medium heat. Add apples and sauté until they begin to brown (about 5 minutes). Add sugar and cinnamon and sauté 3 minutes more. Cool.

CAKE

1½ c all-purpose flour
1 c brown sugar
½ c (1 stick) butter at room temperature and cut into pieces
¾ c persimmon puree
⅓ c sour cream

⅓ c sugar
2 t ginger
¼ c chopped crystallized ginger
1 t baking soda
1 t baking powder
2 large eggs

Preheat oven to 350°. Grease a 9 by 9-inch cake pan. Combine flour, brown sugar, butter and salt in a large bowl. Beat until mixture resembles coarse meal. Set aside 2/3 cup for topping. Add persimmon, sour cream, sugar, and ginger...beating until smooth. Add eggs and mix well. Pour the batter into the pan, scatter apples on top and sprinkle topping over apples. Bake until top is golden brown and tester comes out clean . . . about 1 hour. Serves 6.

FUYU FUJI CRUMBLE WITH GINGER

Crisp Fuyus make an interesting variation on the good old apple crumble. Fujis are my favorite variety of apple, and Fuji Fuyu is fun to say, let alone to eat in this delectable crumble.

3 firm ripe *Fuyu* persimmons
3 *Fuji* apples
2 T candied ginger
1 T lemon juice
1½ t cinnamon

¼ c sugar
½ t salt
½ c chopped dried persimmon (optional)

Toss ingredients in a large mixing bowl. Mound fruit in 9-inch round baking dish. Set aside.

TOPPING

½ c butter in 8 pieces
¾ c packed brown sugar
¾ c flour

½ c chopped pecans
1 egg yolk

Using a food processor with a metal blade, pulse egg yolk with brown sugar, butter, flour, and salt until crumbled and just beginning to come together. Pat topping evenly over fruit to cover, pressing down so it adheres. Scatter pecans over and press them into topping. Bake at 375° until dark brown . . . . about 45 to 50 minutes. Serve warm with whipped topping or ice cream. Makes 6 to 8 servings.

PERSIMMON FLAN

This recipe is a variation on one I found in Cooking Light *magazine. If you cut it into 10 servings, each piece packs only 282 calories of persimmon punch! Not bad for a rich dessert. Be careful when you caramelize the syrup. My first effort crystallized. A drop of something acid – lemon or vinegar – will help prevent this. Cook the syrup until it turns light amber. It will darken as it bakes.*

1½ c sugar	2 egg whites
¼ c water	2 large eggs
½ c persimmon puree	2 c 2% milk
2 T flour	1 t cinnamon
1 block ⅓ less fat cream cheese (8 oz.)	24 thin slices peeled ripe persimmon (about 4 persimmons)

Combine 1 cup sugar and water in a small, heavy saucepan over medium-high heat. Cook until sugar dissolves; stir as needed to dissolve sugar evenly. Cook 9 minutes or until light golden. Immediately pour into a 9-inch round cake pan, tipping quickly so that the syrup coats the bottom of the pan. Preheat your oven to 350°. Combine ½ cup sugar, flour and cinnamon. In a medium sized mixing bowl, beat the cream cheese until smooth, add the flour mixture, mix well and then add the eggs and egg whites. Finally add the milk and persimmon, beating into smooth batter. Pour into your cake pan. Place the cake pan in a broiler pan and add hot water to a depth of 1 inch. Bake at 350° for 1½ hours, or until a knife inserted into the center of the flan comes out clean. Remove cake pan from broiler and cool completely. Chill for 8 hours prior to serving. Loosen edges of flan with a knife. Place a serving plate, upside down, on top of cake pan and invert flan onto plate. Garnish with persimmon slices and serve.

PERSIMMON STREUSEL PIE

This pie features both fresh Fuyus and dried Hachiyas. It takes some effort, but the result is a really unique dessert. Like a brandied Christmas fruit cake, the pie will keep for a couple of weeks. The persimmons should be firm, but as ripe as you can find . . . Fuyus picked in December when they are at their sweetest and most flavorful. This recipe is based on one for fresh pears and originally published in the L.A. Times. I am indebted to my sister Susan who kitchen tested this for me. We both enjoyed the results.

10 dried persimmons
1 c brandy
1 recipe pie crust dough
½ c plus 2 T butter
¼ c whole unblanched almonds
¾ c flour
2-4 c sugar
¾ t salt

¼ c oats
8 large *Fuyu* persimmons
2 T lemon juice
4 star anise
1 2-inch piece of ginger, peeled and sliced into 4 pieces
¼ c light brown sugar

Cover the dried persimmons with brandy and leave overnight. The next day, strain the fruit, reserving the brandy. Quarter the fruit. Roll out the dough and place in a buttered 9- inch pie plate. Trim the edge, leaving ¼ inch beyond the pie plate. Roll the top of the dough up and on top of the edge of the plate. Do not crimp. Refrigerate. Cut 6 tablespoons of butter into half-inch pieces and place in a heavy one-quart pot over medium heat until the butter foams and begins to brown. Remove from the heat, swirl the pot a few times and set aside to cool slightly. Place the almonds in a food processor and grind until fine. Add all the flour, ¼ cup plus 2 tablespoons of sugar and all the salt. Pulse to combine and remove to a bowl. Add the warm butter. And using your hands, toss and squeeze the topping until you have crumb to walnut size pieces. Add the oats and half of the quartered persimmons, toss together and set aside. Peel, halve, and core the fresh persimmons, cut in to quarters and sprinkle with lemon juice.

In a large heavy frying pan, heat 2 tablespoons of butter and 3 tablespoons of sugar until bubbly. Add half the fruit along with 2 star anise and 2 pieces of ginger. Swirl the pan so that the butter and sugar coat the persimmons. Set the pan back on the burner to caramelize the butter and sugar. When the butter begins to brown, swirl the pan to incorporate the browned butter. (The fruit should just begin to soften while the butter and sugar caramelizes.)

Cook the fruit until the cut surfaces are dark golden, about 12 minutes. If the butter browns too quickly, lower the heat.

Remove the pan from the heat and add 2 tablespoons of the reserved brandy. Return the pan to the heat, gently swirl and reduce the liquid until a spoonful poured over a persimmon sticks slightly. Remove the persimmons to a large bowl, scraping the caramel sauce over them. Discard the star anise and ginger. Wash the pan and repeat the above process with the remaining fruit. Heat the oven to 350°. Put all of the caramelized fruit in the mixing bowl, then add the brown sugar and ground sugar as well as the remaining dried persimmons and toss together. Crimp the edge of your pie crust and place the filling in the shell and sprinkle the streusel over the top. Bake the whole elaborate production for 1 hour and 45 minutes, or until any liquid bubbling is a dark caramel color. Serve with pride and some whipped cream.

GINGER PERSIMMON CHEESECAKE WITH SOUR CREAM TOPPING

This is a variation of a cheesecake recipe shared with me many years ago by a college roommate. As cheesecakes go, it's easy to make and a little lighter than most. The persimmon gives it a gorgeous color.

CRUST

1 c graham or gingersnap crumbs
¼ c sugar
5 T melted butter

1 t cinnamon (omit if you're using the gingersnaps)

Grease a 9-inch pie plate and pat this mixture into it. Set aside.

FILLING

3 eggs
1 c sugar
½ c strained persimmon pulp (2 persimmons)
2 T flour
1 t ground ginger
1½ packages light cream cheese, at room temperature (12 oz.)
1 t vanilla
¼ t salt

Whirl eggs, sugar, flour, ginger, cream cheese and persimmon in a food processor until smooth. Then pour into prepared crust. Bake in a 350° oven for 40 minutes or until firm. Remove from oven and let cool for 10 minutes. In the meantime mix:

TOPPING

1 c light sour cream
5 T sugar
1 t vanilla
1 T persimmon pulp

Carefully pour this mixture over the top of the cheesecake – smoothing it out with a spatula. Return to oven for 10 minutes. Remove, let cool, and then chill for at least 4 hours. Serves 8 to 10 lucky people.

STUFFED DRIED PERSIMMONS

These are based on a stuffed date recipe in Deborah Madison's cookbook The Savory Way. *Much to my surprise, I found that almond paste is readily available at any supermarket, even our small Ojai Vons. These are very simple to make, fun to serve and just delicious. Almond paste was one of my good friend Dorothy Rail's favorite confections. She loved these.*

10 or so dried persimmons
20 slivered almonds
A tube of almond paste

If the persimmons are hard or dry, set them in a steamer over boiling water until they've softened, 3 to 5 minutes. Let them cool for a few minutes. Cut the persimmons in two, and with a sharp knife, carefully remove the central core, discard or feed this to the cook. Check for any seeds and remove them as well. Squeeze a bit of almond paste into the cavity and top with a slivered almond. Arrange on a tray...perhaps with some persimmon cookies, and serve.

PERSIMMON SORBET

This one appeared in a Los Angeles Times *article on spa food. Each serving has only 64 calories . . . so this is a very light treat. It's also very pretty and refreshing.*

8 persimmons, cut into large dice	¾ c water
1 c sugar	1 t lemon juice

Puree the persimmons in a food processor and strain the puree. Set aside. Make simple syrup by boiling water with sugar until the sugar dissolves, about 1 minute. Measure out ½ cup. Combine the simple syrup and lemon juice. Add to puree and mix well. Freeze the puree in an ice cream maker according to the manufacturer's directions. The result will be a soft, creamy sorbet.

PERSIMMON ICE CREAM

Another Los Angeles Times *entry in the persimmon dessert derby. This one could become a favorite of yours. My sister Susan spotted this and tried it out first. It's very pretty and fairly easy to make.*

1 c strained persimmon puree	¾ c sugar
½ t cinnamon	2 c half & half
¼ t ground ginger	

In a medium sized mixing bowl, stir together persimmon puree and spices. Chill mixture at least 4 hours. Add sugar and stir until dissolved, about 3 minutes. Combine persimmon mixture and half-and-half in ice cream maker and process according to manufacturer's directions until set. You'll end up with 1 quart of unique persimmon ice cream . . . about 6 servings.

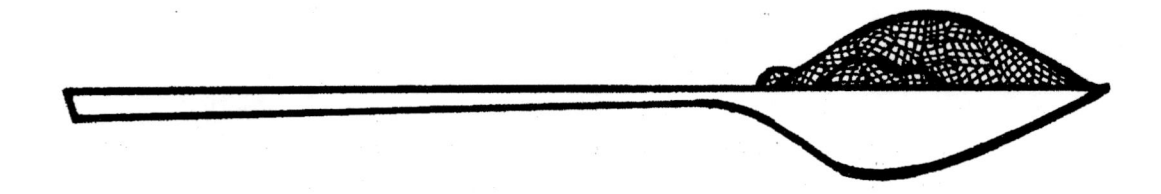

LOW-CALORIE PERSIMMON WHIP

If you're counting calories and long for something sweet, consider trying this whip. It's based on a recipe I remember appeared in Sunset magazine years ago. The amounts given are only enough for one serving. You can increase them if you wish.

⅓ c nonfat milk
⅓ c instant nonfat milk solids
Either 1 t honey or 1 serving stevia

½ t cinnamon
2 T persimmon puree

Pour nonfat milk into a small metal mixing bowl and put the bowl in your freezer for about 20 minutes. Ice crystals should form on the edges of the milk. Chill the beaters from your mixer as well. Using a hand held mixer, beat non-fat milk solids into non-fat milk. Continue to beat on high until soft peaks form, about two minutes. Add cinnamon and sweetener and continue to beat for another 2 minutes. Stir in persimmon, pour into serving bowl and enjoy. You must eat the whip right away. It begins to separate fairly quickly.

BRENDA LOREE'S MOM FERN'S PERSIMMON PUDDING

Like my mom, Fern was from Missouri...and cooks in Missouri are raised right . . . they know their pie crust and their persimmon pudding too.

1 beaten egg
Pinch of salt
1 c sugar
1 c flour
½ c milk

1 t cinnamon
¼ t cloves
2 t soda
1 c mashed persimmon
Melted butter the size of an egg

Mix dry ingredients, then add egg, milk and persimmons. Grease casserole with butter. Add ingredients to casserole and set in pan of hot water in oven. Bake 2 hours at 350°. Top with the following sauce. Serve warm.

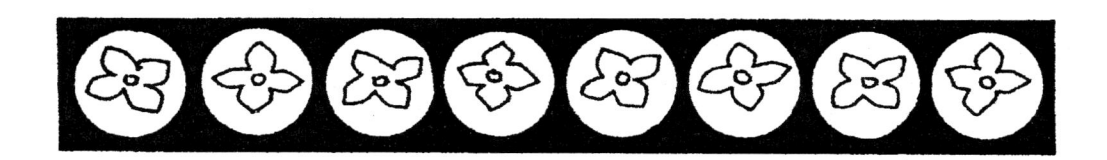

SAUCE FOR THE TOP

1 beaten egg
½ c powdered sugar
1 c whipping cream
Pinch of vanilla
Pinch of nutmeg

Add powdered sugar to beaten egg. Whip whipping cream very stiff. Blend all and add vanilla and nutmeg.

SUNSET'S PERSIMMON INDIAN PUDDING

1 c persimmon puree
2 t baking soda
¾ c sugar
½ c butter
¼ c dark molasses
2 large eggs
1 t vanilla
1 c all purpose flour
¾ c cornmeal
½ t each ginger and cinnamon
¼ t allspice
1 c raisins
½ c chopped walnuts

Stir persimmon pulp with soda and set aside. Beat together sugar, butter and molasses until blended. Add eggs and vanilla and beat until smooth. In a separate bowl, stir flour with cornmeal, cinnamon, ginger and allspice. Gradually stir into batter along with puree, raisins and nuts. Pour into a buttered 6 to 7 cup loaf pan or ring mold. (No deeper than 3 inches.) Cover tightly with foil. Put pan in a larger pan and place in 300° oven. To larger pan, add ¾ inches boiling water around loaf pan or ½ inches water around ring mold. Bake until pudding is firm in center when lightly pressed (about 2 hours). Let stand 10 minutes, then run a knife around side of pan to release. Serve with whipped cream or syllabub sauce. Makes 12 servings.

PERSIMMON SYLLABUB SAUCE

2 c persimmon puree – strained
1 c whipping cream
1 c powdered sugar
⅓ c dry sherry
2 t lemon juice

With an electric mixer, whip cream and sugar until mixture will hold soft peaks. Stir in persimmon puree, sherry and lemon juice to taste. Serve or cover and chill up to 1 day. To serve as dessert, stir and spoon into small bowls or use as a topping for cake.

PERSIMMON FLUMMERY

Another interesting recipe I got from my neighbor Susan Baldwin.

1 T gelatin	1 c persimmon pulp (strained)
½ c water	1 t vanilla extract
½ c sugar	4 egg whites
3 T lemon juice	Dash of salt

Sprinkle the gelatin into half the water. Let sit for 2 minutes. Bring remaining water to a boil and stir in the gelatin and sugar until dissolved. Stir in the lemon juice. Cool 10 minutes then add the persimmon and vanilla. Chill until mixture looks syrupy. Beat the egg whites until stiff. Beat the chilled persimmon mixture until frothy, then combine with stiff egg whites and beat until mixture holds its shape. Turn into mold and chill 4 hours. Serves 6 to 8.

RUM SOAKED DRIED PERSIMMONS

I love the flavor of rum, and it occurred to me that a dousing of this might be a good fate for very dry dried persimmons. . .those you may have left too long in your drying shed. I have been guilty of this from time to time. The rum marinade works beautifully at reviving some old desiccated fruit and it's a simple trick. Try it with other liqueurs as well . . . triple sec or Pernod or sake. Each has possibilities.

6 dried persimmons	⅓ c brown sugar
⅔ c rum	Zest of two oranges

In a small sauce pan bring the rum to a low boil and add the sugar, stir until it dissolves and add the orange peel. Remove from heat. Quarter each dried persimmon. Prick the persimmons 4 or 5 times with a fork so they'll absorb the flavor better. Place them in a small dish and pour the rum over. Let marinate overnight in the refrigerator. These keep indefinitely.

AND NOW,

THE COOKIES!

AND NOW, THE COOKIES!

PERSIMMON GINGER COOKIES

6 T butter at room temperature	1 t baking soda
1½ c sugar	Pinch of salt
1 egg	¼ c persimmon puree (1 persimmon)
2 c flour	1 to 2 T chopped preserved ginger (optional)
1½ t ground ginger	

In a medium sized bowl, cream the butter and 1 cup of the sugar. Add the egg and beat well. Then add the persimmon puree and the preserved ginger. In a separate bowl, sift the dry ingredients and add them to the cookie batter. Refrigerate the batter for at least 1 hour. It will be easier to work with. Preheat oven to 350° and grease cookie sheets. Shape cookies by rolling dough into approximately 1-inch balls by hand. Dip them in sugar and place on baking sheets. Flatten with the prongs of a fork dipped into water so it won't stick in the dough. Bake for 12 to 15 minutes. Makes about 36 small cookies.

DRIED PERSIMMON BARS

About 12 dried persimmons, chopped (enough to make two cups)	1 c flour
2 c brown sugar	1 c oatmeal
1 c water	½ t baking soda
1 t vanilla	¼ t salt
Zest of two oranges	½ c butter (1 stick)

In a large saucepan combine persimmons, 1 cup brown sugar, water and orange peel and vanilla. Bring to a boil, turn heat down and simmer for 2 minutes. Cool, and puree in a food processor. Set aside. Place flour, 1 cup brown sugar, baking soda, and salt in the food processor. Pulse to combine. Then add chunks of cold butter until mixture is crumbly. Pat half of mixture into greased 9-by-12 inch baking pan. Cover with persimmon mixture. Top with remaining crumb mixture. Press down lightly.

Bake at 350° until top is golden brown – about 35 to 40 minutes. Cool before cutting into squares. Makes about 18.

MOSTLY DEBORAH MADISON'S DELICIOUS PERSIMMON BARS

Deborah Madison is the splendid cook who wrote The Savory Way, *one of my favorite cookbooks. This is a variation of her recipe. It makes a pretty cookie . . . full of surprises.*

1 c dried currants	1 c sugar
1¾ c unbleached white flour - sifted	2 t lemon juice
	1 egg
1 t cinnamon	½ c melted butter or canola cooking oil
½ t salt	
1 c persimmon pulp	1 c chopped walnuts or pecans
1 t baking soda	¼ c chopped preserved ginger

Preheat the oven to 350°. Grease and flour a 10-by-14 inch baking pan. If the currants are dry and hard, cover them with warm water and set them aside while you get the other ingredients. Combine the flour with the cinnamon and salt in one bowl. In another bowl, combine the persimmon puree and baking soda and beat until smooth, then add lemon juice, egg, sugar and melted butter. Mix well. Add the dry ingredients to the batter. Drain the currents and add them along with the nuts and the chopped ginger. Spread the batter over the pan and bake until firm and lightly brown on top, about 25 to 30 minutes. Let cool and then dribble with lemon glaze or use one of the frostings included in the cake recipes...cream cheese is good. This recipe makes about 24 bars.

LEMON GLAZE

Juice of 1 lemon	1 c powdered sugar

Stir enough juice into the sugar to make it the texture of thick cream.

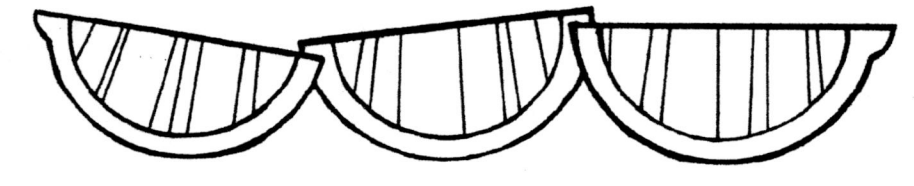

OATMEAL RAISIN PERSIMMON COOKIES

1 c raisins	1½ c flour
1 c butter	1 t salt
1 c sugar	1 t baking soda
1 c brown sugar	1½ c persimmon puree
3 T milk	2 c rolled oats
2 t vanilla	

Cover raisins with water in a small saucepan and bring to a boil. Turn off heat and let stand for a bit . . . then drain off the water. In a large mixing bowl, cream the butter, eggs, sugar, milk and vanilla. Mix the dry ingredients in another bowl, and then add them to the batter. Beat in the raisins, persimmons and oatmeal. Spoon on to greased cookie sheets and bake at 375° for about 10 minutes, removing cookies from the oven when they are still soft. Cool before removing from the pan. Makes about 30 cookies.

JOY OF COOKING BUTTERSCOTCH BROWNIES
WITH A PERSIMMON TWIST

My school cafeteria used to serve a cookie very similar to these. I was a great fan then and remain one. They are very tempting, but if you can resist, they keep beautifully in the freezer. I often double the recipe. And reluctantly give them away(!). For a cookie with a real flair, consider using the rum soaked dried persimmons I've described elsewhere in the cookbook.

¼ c butter	½ t salt
1 c brown sugar	½ c chopped pecans
1 egg	2 T chopped crystallized ginger
1 t vanilla	(optional but delicious)
½ c all-purpose flour	½ c chopped dried persimmon
1 t baking powder	

Melt the butter in a saucepan, add the sugar and stir. Keep stirring just until the mixture bubbles, about 2 minutes. Remove from heat and let cool a bit. In a separate bowl, sift the dry ingredients together. Add half of this to the sugar mixture along with the vanilla. Now beat in the egg and then add the remaining ingredients. Mix well and then scrape the dough into a well-greased 9-by-9 inch dish and bake at 350° for 25 minutes.

PERSIMMON JAM CRESCENTS

These are based on a fig cookie recipe. I'm not too skilled working with pastry, but these are worth the fumbling effort. The filling is wonderful and is a treat to make just in itself.

PERSIMMON JAM FILLING

12 dried persimmons
1 c sugar
1 c water
1 T lemon zest
2 T lemon juice

Cut the persimmons into half-inch pieces (check for seeds). Put them in a medium saucepan with the sugar, the water, lemon zest and lemon juice. Bring to a boil and then reduce the heat to medium and cook, stirring often until the liquid is reduced to a syrup, about 5 to 6 minutes. If mixture gets too thick, add a little water. Cool slightly, then place in a food processor and puree.

COOKIES

2¼ c flour
¼ c sugar
¼ t salt
1 c (2 sticks) butter, cut into ½-inch pieces, chilled
8 ounces cream cheese, cut into ½-inch pieces, chilled
2 T sour cream

Place the flour, sugar and salt into a food processor and pulse to combine. Add the butter, cream cheese, and sour cream and process until a crumbly dough forms, about 20 to 30 seconds. Spoon the dough onto a work surface and form into a round. Cut the dough into four equal pieces. Make a ball out of each piece and wrap tightly in plastic wrap. Refrigerate until firm, about 25 minutes. Heat the oven to 375° and grease 3 baking sheets. Roll out one round of dough on a lightly floured surface to form about a 9-inch circle. If cracks form along the edges, push the dough back together to form a relatively even edge. Spread a quarter of the fruit jam to within a half inch of the edge, then using a sharp knife, cut the round into 8 triangles. Form the cookies by rolling up each triangle towards the center. Place each set of cookies on the baking sheet and repeat each process with each round. Bake until golden brown – about 20 minutes. The cookies are best the first day, but will keep in the freezer for up to 3 months.

DOROTHY RAIL'S WONDERFUL PERSIMMON COOKIES

In my end is my beginning. This is the recipe that got me started on the persimmon highway.

½ c persimmon pulp (1 persimmon, mashed)
1 c sugar
½ c butter (1 stick)
1 egg
1½ c flour

½ t salt
1 t cinnamon
½ t nutmeg
½ t cloves
1 t baking soda
1 c raisins

In a large mixing bowl, beat egg with butter. Add sugar and persimmon and mix well . . . then add dry ingredients. Mix in raisins and drop by spoonfuls onto greased cookie sheet. Bake at 350° for about 15 minutes.

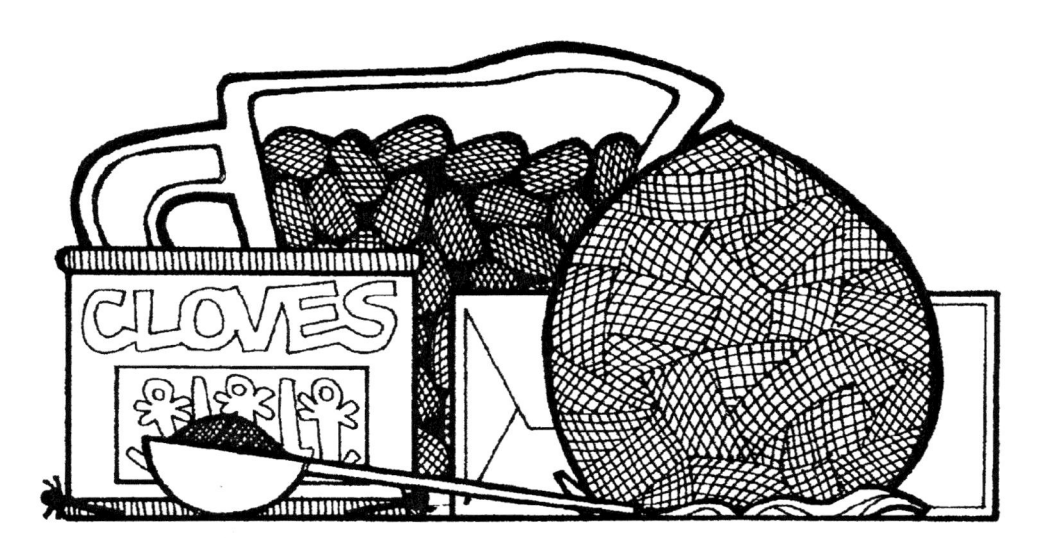

ACKNOWLEDGMENTS

Many people have helped and encouraged me with this little book, especially my sister Susan Bee and friends Sally Hoover, Sue Mills, Dixie Adeniran, Lynn Lykins and Karen McAuley. I typed part of the manuscript at Kim Armstrong's little house in Mexico. Yes it's finally done Kim! My husband Jim tasted everything and kept the computer alive. This book is for him and for my late friend Dorothy Rail, who got me started.

ABOUT THE AUTHOR

Ann Crozier-Duke could easily pass as your stereotypical librarian. She had the glasses, the stylish yet sensible hairdo, the soft voice (usually) and even the rather sensible shoes.

But those who would judge a librarian by her bifocals would have done well to peer behind the lenses. They camouflaged a pair of eyes that fully lived up to that tritest of terms, "a twinkle in her eye." No kidding, they actually twinkled.

And when they did, it meant something good was about to happen. Ann was (A) about to put a book in your hands she'd picked out just for you – the one you came to the library hoping to find. Or (B) she'd just thought of some colorful witticism to tell you in that soft voice – a witticism that would make a sailor blush.

Ann was bashful, she was bawdy, she was serious, she was shy. She was certainly no snob. She had a sensibility that could refine a new recipe for a delicately-seasoned persimmon soup. She could discern just which Jane Austen novel a young woman should start with. And she gleefully sensed when you were in the mood to go home and curl up with a gory serial killer police procedural.

She hosted luncheons in her Ojai home which is surrounded by persimmon and avocado trees. And yes, her meals would always feature new persimmon dishes. She unabashedly exploited her friends and patrons as guinea pigs for her new recipes. All of us guinea pigs would go home as unusually happy guinea pigs too, asking on the way out when we might return as subjects for her next experiment.

– Brenda Nell Loree

ABOUT THE AUTHOR ~ BY THE AUTHOR

In 2007, Ann attended a six-week Neighborhood Hospice Seminar sponsored by Help of Ojai. One of the homework assignments was to write a personal obituary. The obituary was to be written, not for class sharing, but as a personal exercise. Here's what Ann wrote:

Ann Bell Crozier died recently while happily eating one of her favorite foods: a tuna sandwich. Born in 1945 in Missouri, Ann was fortunate enough to have as parents John and Mary Bell, who gave her a love of reading, animals, friends and family. The Bells moved to Honolulu, Hawaii in 1947, just after taking Ann to the Mayo clinic for treatment of her eyes. Doctors there wanted to remove them, but her father, a young doctor, decided against this recommendation. This was an experience that gave Ann a healthy skepticism about medical treatment for the rest of her life.

Ann graduated from UC Berkeley and married David Crozier, also of Honolulu. They moved to California and discovered Ojai, at that time a small dusty town full of hippies, artists and spiritual seekers. They both loved it.

Ann went to UCLA, got an MLS degree and went to work for Ventura County as a librarian. She ran the Ojai Library for 26 years and retired at the ripe young age of 54.

She lost Dave in 1990, met Jim Duke, a retired newspaper editor, in 1997. Together they read many books, watched a lot of wildlife and foreign films and tended a scraggly but well-loved garden of California native plants and wildflowers.

Ann wrote a cookbook and memoir entitled, *Passion for Persimmons.*

She is hopefully survived by her partner Jim, sister Susan and brother John, two nephews and two stepsons. Donations in her name may be sent to the Ojai Library and the Ventura Audubon Society. If you choose to donate something to the library, tell the staff that the purchase of more cookbooks might indeed be appropriate . . . perhaps something on comfort foods?

ABOUT THE ILLUSTRATOR

Illustrations for *Passion for Persimmons* were done by Beverly Armstrong, a patron of the Ojai Library since 1950, as a "gift back" to that beloved institution for its influence on her life.

RECIPE INDEX

APPETIZERS, 13-20

    Alternate turnover filling featuring fennel and anise, 19

    Dried persimmons with goat cheese, 15

    Fresh fuyu persimmons with lime, 15

    Open-faced cheese, onion and roasted persimmon sandwiches, 19

    Persimmon hummus, 16

    Persimmon pâté, 17

    Persimmon pickles, 16

    Persimmon spring rolls with peanut sauce, 20

    Roasted persimmon turnovers with allspice and orange, 17

BREADS, 21-29

    Dried persimmon nut bread, 28

    High fiber low fat persimmon nut bread, 29

    Onion persimmon bread with a surprise, 26

    Orange almond persimmon bread, 24

    Orange persimmon rolls, 27

    Persimmon anise bread, 23

    Persimmon bread with cinnamon and raisins, 25

    Persimmon corn muffins, 28

    Persimmon ginger bread, 25

    Persimmon muffins, 27

COOKIES, 80-85

Dorothy Rail's wonderful persimmon cookies, 85

Dried persimmon bars, 81

Joy of Cooking butterscotch brownies with a persimmon twist, 83

Mostly Deborah Madison's delicious persimmon bars, 82

Oatmeal raisin persimmon cookies, 83

Persimmon ginger cookies, 81

Persimmon jam crescents, 84

DESSERTS, 64-77

Brenda Loree's Mom Fern's persimmon pudding, 75

Chocolate persimmon cake with orange zest, 65

Cream cheese icing, 65

Fuyu bundt cake, 68

Fuyu fuji crumble with ginger, 69

Ginger persimmon cheesecake with sour cream topping, 72

Low-calorie persimmon whip, 75

Persimmon anise cake, 67

Persimmon apple streusel cake, 68

Persimmon cake with rum orange icing, 66

Persimmon carrot cake, 66

Persimmon flan, 70

Persimmon flummery, 77

Persimmon ice cream, 74

Persimmon sorbet, 74

Persimmon streusel pie, 71

Persimmon syllabub sauce, 76

Rum orange icing, 67

Rum soaked dried persimmons, 77

Stuffed dried persimmons, 73

Sunset's persimmon Indian pudding, 76

PERSIMMONS, INTRODUCTION AND PROCESSING, 7-12

Drying, 10

Processing, 9

Roasting, 11

SALADS AND SALAD DRESSINGS, 41-55

Apple persimmon molded salad, 54

Braised red cabbage, onion and persimmon salad, 49

Dried persimmon, orange and fennel salad with pomegranates and anise, 51

Fresh fuyu persimmon, avocado and spinach salad, 50

Mixed green salad with fuyu persimmons and raspberry persimmon vinaigrette, 44

Molded persimmon salad with cottage cheese, ginger and other weird things, 53

Mustard vinaigrette, 48

Ojai Waldorf salad with fresh fuyu, 52

Persimmon fruit salad with tamarind, 46

Persimmon, jicama and cucumber salad, 43

Persimmon mayonnaise with orange, 54

Persimmon miso mayonnaise, 55

Persimmon soy citrus dressing, 55

Persimmon yogurt molded salad, 52

Pineapple persimmon vinaigrette, 55

Roasted dried persimmon salad with goat cheese, 45

Roasted fuyu persimmon potato salad with lemon and rosemary, 47

Roasted fuyu potato salad with cumin and lime, 46

Roasted persimmon salad with roasted carrots and cinnamon, 48

Salad, 45

Still another roasted persimmon salad . . . this one with cauliflower, 48

SAUCES, SALSAS, CHUTNEYS, AND JAMS, 57-62

Cranberry persimmon relish, 61

Fuyu persimmon chutney, 60

Fuyu salsa, 62

Persimmon freezer jam, 62

Pesimmon miso sauce, 59

Persimmon salsa no. 2, 62

Persimmon tamarind sauce, 59

Sunset's Apricot persimmon chutney for either hachiya or fuyu 'simmons, 60

SOUPS, 31-39

    Ann's 'simmons minestrone, 35

    Chilled persimmon soup with pineapple and rum, 39

    Cold persimmon bisque with orange juice and cinnamon, 39

    Hot and mostly sour persimmon soup with tofu and mushrooms, 36

    Mainlining vitamin A curried carrot and persimmon soup, 38

    Persimmon chicken soup, 33

    Roasted fuyu persimmon soup with red miso paste, 33

    Roasted persimmon black bean soup with cumin, 37

    Roasted persimmon soup with lemon grass and white beans, 37

    Sweet mama roasted persimmon soup with star anise, 36

    Thai persimmon peanut soup, 34